The Magic of Grandparenting

Foreword by

Cathryn Girard

President,
Caring Grandparents of America

The Magic of Grandparenting

Charmaine L. Ciardi, Ed.D.
Cathy Nikkel Orme
Carolyn Quatrano

An Owl Book

Henry Holt and Company
New York

Henry Holt and Company, Inc.
Publishers since 1866
115 West 18th Street
New York, New York 10011

Henry Holt® is a registered
trademark of Henry Holt and Company, Inc.

Published in Canada by Fitzhenry & Whiteside Ltd.,
195 Allstate Parkway, Markham, Ontario L3R 4T8.

Library of Congress Cataloging-in-Publication Data
Ciardi, Charmaine L.
The magic of grandparenting / Charmaine L. Ciardi, Cathy Nikkel
Orme, Carolyn Quatrano; with a foreword by Cathryn Girard.
       p.   cm.
1. Grandparenting.   2. Grandparent and child.   I. Orme, Cathy
       Nikkel.   II. Quatrano, Carolyn.   III. Title.
HQ759.9.C5   1995   95-7679
306.874'5—dc20   CIP

ISBN 0-8050-4075-7 (An Owl book: pbk.)

Henry Holt books are available for special promotions and
premiums. For details contact: Director, Special Markets.

First Owl Book Edition—1995

Designed by Kate Nichols

Printed in the United States of America
All first editions are printed on acid-free paper. ∞

1   3   5   6   9   10   8   6   4   2

In celebration of our families,
who continue to give both
meaning and magic to life.

Contents

Foreword

*F*or countless adults some of their most treasured childhood memories are of experiences shared with a grandparent. In recent years I have made it a habit to ask people
about their grandparents. Almost universally, before they
even begin to respond with words, a broad smile comes
across their faces. That's the *magic of grandparenting*. It is a
legacy of the best kind of love because it is given with
little, if any, thought to what the giver will get in return.

The stories these adults go on to tell are always filled
with great emotion and high drama, in spite of the fact
that the stuff of the story may be as simple as a box of
buttons, a longed-for doll or truck, a favorite story read till
the book's pages became tattered, or a peanut butter and
jelly sandwich—you wouldn't believe the number of ways

a grandparent can turn peanut butter and jelly into gourmet fare. The point is that to a child the common, ordinary events of life become special when they come with the wholehearted love and attention of an adult who for that moment has given herself completely to that child. That is the essence of grandparenting.

It is fitting that this book is being published in 1995 because on October 14, 1994, the President of the United States signed into law Senate Joint Resolution 198, designating 1995 the Year of the Grandparent. This resolution calls upon the people of the United States to observe the year with appropriate programs, ceremonies, and activities. What better way to be a part of this grand year dedicated to grandparents than with the publication of this very special book.

So what of grandparenting in the '90s and beyond? First of all, there are over sixty million grandparents in the United States today, representing more than thirty-one percent of the U.S. adult population. By the year 2000 that number will swell to sixty-nine million, with the largest growth—a thirty-three percent increase—coming from adults who will be between the ages of 45 and 59. This tremendous growth spurt is being fueled by the aging of the baby boom generation, which begins to turn 50 in 1996, and by the fact that the average woman becomes a first-time grandmother between the ages of 45 and 50. Therefore, the influence of grandparents today and into the future is consequential—baby boomers have influenced every stage of life through which they have moved. So what shall we expect from and to what shall we exhort this grand group of mature Americans in their role as grandparents?

First of all, the image of grandparents is changing and will continue to change. No longer do the people in the picture have only white hair, conservative clothes, and objects from the home in their hands. The reality has been changing gradually, but as a society we are reluctant to let go of our stereotypical images. Indeed, grandparents and grandparenting has changed over the last thirty years just as America's families have changed.

Few would deny that these changes have often put families under severe stress, whether it be economic, social, or personal. Support systems taken for granted only a generation ago—school, church, community, and extended family—are no longer as readily available to help parents raise their children. But it's not all gloom and doom. In fact, there is so much that is good going on among grandparents and their families that we decided back in 1992 to form an organization whose mission would be to recognize and reward grandparents and to celebrate grandparenting. That organization, Caring Grandparents of America (CGA), is over 300,000 strong and growing.

There is an ancient Chinese proverb that says: "The greatest gifts a parent can bestow upon a child are roots and wings." CGA promotes a partnership between parents and grandparents for the purpose of deepening every child's roots and strengthening every child's wings so that he or she may soar into adulthood with a glad heart and a confident spirit. How can this be accomplished? Through understanding and sharing among the generations.

This is what *The Magic of Grandparenting* is all about. The book doesn't shy away from the changes that have occurred since today's grandparents were parenting, but it inspires them to hold on to the best of the past and enrich their new families with all the specialness that only grandparents can bring to a family and to grandchildren. We see from the anecdotes liberally sprinkled throughout the text that the smallest incidents can and still do make the greatest impressions. This book is a celebration of the unique role of grandparents in the family, and it encourages grandparents to keep up the good work and to find ways to adapt time-honored traditions to the complexities of today's families—and to remember that truly the best gift they can give to their grandchildren is the gift of themselves.

The authors of *The Magic of Grandparenting* each bring a special approach to the subject of grandparenting. Charmaine Ciardi brings experiences both from a rich family life and from her work as a professional dealing with family relationships. Love is always visible in the professional advice and counseling she gives to so many and in the column she writes for *Grandparent Times*, the signature publication of Caring Grandparents of America.

Cathy Orme and Carolyn Quatrano, writers, editors, and moms, each have taken a special interest in grandparenting based on their own experiences with grandparents and grandchildren. Their sensitivity to the importance of this relationship to children shines through.

It is my pleasure to be a part of bringing this unique story about the magic of grandparenting to families everywhere.

Cathryn C. Girard
Founder and President,
Caring Grandparents of America

Acknowledgments

The authors wish to thank all of those who so generously shared their grandparent stories with us. Although only some of these memories are quoted in the text, all of them influenced the tone and direction of the book.

Introduction

$\mathcal{N}$ana, Grampy, Bubbie, Verade, Mimi, Poppie—no matter what we're called, grandparents are special. Grandparents come in all sizes, shapes, and colors and share many differences in ideas, politics, religions, customs, and traditions. Grandparents are definitely not a predictable class of people acting out a ritual role. Grandparental unity comes from a dream we all share: that our children and grandchildren live full, happy, and productive lives.

Throughout history, grandparents have had an active part in making that dream a reality. We were children when we first knew our grandparents, and they were wonderful in our eyes. But in our childish vision, we also saw them as "old." Probably they were no older than we are now. It is this lingering childhood perception that may make us rebel slightly when we hear the news that we are going to be a grandparent. "I don't want to be called Grandma, I'm not that old," may be our first response. Jettison childhood perceptions. Grandparenting is for those who live life to the fullest. It is a rejuvenating relationship with a brand-new human being who will explore the world with us in wonder and excitement.

As a society wrestling with today's many changes in the fabric of family, we are beginning to rediscover just how important grandparents are—not only to the health of the family but to the health of the country.

Most of us become grandparents sooner or later. Although some attain this distinction while still in their thirties and others not until their fifties, most first-time grandparents are in their forties. Today's grandparents are in the prime of life, near the top of their careers, and in good health. We are better educated and more economically secure than previous generations, and are health, nutrition, and exercise conscious. In short, grandparents are active, energetic people, and our grandchildren need us.

From the very beginning, grandparents have held a special place in heart and home. Yet from a historical perspective, the grandparenting role has undergone an upheaval in recent decades that is without precedent. The '60s revolution changed much of American social thought and altered in a fundamental but subtle way the perception and role of grandparents. The philosophy of "Never trust anyone over thirty" and "If it feels good, do it" meant a double whammy for grandparents. No longer did wisdom equate with experience. Youth and young thought were exalted at the expense of the previous generation. At the same time, a profound skepticism of traditional values and practices caused young people to reject those very principles that were the guiding lights of their grandparents.

℘ "A great many grandparents have given up emotional attachments to their grandchildren. They have ceded the power to determine their grandparenting relationships to the grandchildren's parents and, in effect, have turned their backs on an entire generation."

—Arthur Kornhaber,
Grandparents, Grandchildren:
A Vital Connection

During the '70s and '80s we wrestled with new roles in the family. Women left home in droves for the workplace. Men discovered nurturing. Inflation and consumerism made two-income families the norm. Children spent more waking hours in day care than they did at home. Job scarcity and industrial downsizing made experienced workers easy targets for premature retirement. Skyrocketing rates of divorce and unwed parenthood translated into children growing up with one parent who almost always had to work.

Recognizing the risky position of families and most

especially of children, state and federal governments and a host of other organizations devised a potpourri of programs to help. Family support programs spun off family preservation programs; mentor and tutor programs spawned a variety of linkage arrangements between generations.

Along the way, policy implementers noticed that the children hungry for adult attention far outnumbered the available mentors. This realization led them to the conclusion that help would have to come from the previous generation—grandparents. This was realized at the state and local levels. As a consequence, a wide array of intergenerational programs evolved that recruited surrogate or foster grandparents to develop a grand relationship with hard-pressed kids. Where they were supported, these programs worked. They linked children in schools, recreation programs, day care settings, health centers, camps, and juvenile detention facilities to caring volunteer or paid grandparents. Grandparents were rediscovered. Once again, we were seen as filling a unique role in a family unit, whether we were related by blood or human caring.

In the '90s, we are witnessing a resurgence of interest in grandparenting and, most especially, in the unique power inherent in the grandparent–grandchild relationship. This renaissance in the value and potential of grandparenting is occurring across the land. In discovering the mystique of grandparenting, the U.S. Congress passed legislation in October 1994 designating 1995 as the Year of the Grandparent.

Not all grandparents are wonderful or memorable. But when grandparenting really works, a relationship is forged that influences not only this family but also succeeding generations. American Indians have always believed that when they grandparent a child, they are nurturing not just one child but seven generations yet unborn. The rewards of grandparenting extend beyond a special relationship with one child and well into the future. It is a relationship that should never be missed or dismissed. Anyone who tries can become a legendary grandparent. We have nothing to lose and everything to gain.

Freed of all the parental aspects of teaching and disciplining, the grandparent and grandchild can explore the world together at their own pace. Even separated by oceans or continents, grandparents and grandchildren can reach out and enjoy a mutually enhancing relationship. Commitment and love are the essential ingredients. While a grandchild gains self-esteem and security from a relationship that focuses solely on his individual personality and potential, the grandparent gains personal fulfillment and a shot at immortality.

Although each grandparent is unique, there are some generalizations that can be used to outline a successful grandparent. Wonderful grandparents are those who

- rejoice in their children's adult status and seek a continuing relationship with their children and grandchildren;

- are willing to commit time to their relationships;
- do not try to control people;
- can accept change as inevitable and healthy;
- enjoy the adventure of life;
- see and comment on what is good in others;
- are good listeners;
- are good negotiators;
- give without expectation of return;
- are fun to be around; and
- like all kinds of people.

Above all else, the magic ingredient in a successful grandparenting relationship is unconditional love. Love this child because she is your grandchild. Treasure her individuality, curiosity, wonder, and unique personality.

The chapters that follow illuminate the best of grandparenting under the best and most trying of circumstances. If they serve to increase your anticipation and joy in this most special of life's stages, then our goal has been met. We invite you to discover the magic of grandparenting.

Enjoy.

1

Once Upon a Time

❖

Discovering the Magic in a Grandparenting Relationship

Grandparents can create magic. It makes no difference who we are. Just like Jack, we sowed and tended seeds that sprouted and grew and now offer the stairway to a magic world. Magic happens when grandparent and grandchild together step outside the everyday world and enclose each other in a world of their own where adventure, discovery, and exploration are commonplace.

What do you remember most about your grandparents? Almost everyone has the same reaction to that question. A smile begins and grows until it is big and warm. Then, without hesitation, comes the sharing of a cherished memory of good times spent with a very special person— quiet teas, fishing trips, building a fortress together, berry picking, storytelling, snowball fights, companionship.

*T*IP: Underscore how important the grandparent–grandchild relationship can be by sharing the best or strongest memories of your own grandparents with this new generation.

✍ "My grandparents always loved me because I was me. Through good times and bad, no matter what I had done, however miserable my mood, they were always there for me. They would do anything for me. And I would do anything for them."

—Jeanne, age 30

Being a grandparent has nothing to do with being bored, having too much time on our hands, walking with a cane, or having silver hair. It is not for the weary but for the adventuresome, the imaginative, and the wise.

The potential for magic is in our relationship with each grandchild presented to us. We can grab the opportunity to expand ourselves and the world around us or refuse it, remain unchanged, and lose forever a unique part of our lives.

---

*T*IP: Resurrect the fondest memories of family times from your childhood and tailor them to this generation. Cut down a Christmas tree together, make fudge on a wintry evening, build a fort together . . .

✍ "Grandparents are our continuing tie to the near-past, to the events and beliefs and experiences that so strongly affect our lives and the world around us. Whether they are our own or surrogate grandparents who fill some of the gaps in our mobile society, our senior generation also provides our society a link to our national heritage and traditions.

"We all know grandparents whose values transcend passing fads and pressures and who possess the wisdom of distilled pain and joy. Because they are usually free to love and guide and befriend the young without having to take daily responsibility for them, they can often reach out past pride and fear of failure and close the space between generations."

—President Jimmy Carter, September 6, 1979

Grandparenting is a relationship so special that adults who knew the power and pleasure of it as children carry it as one of their talismans against the slings and arrows of the outside world. The aroma of a certain food, the style of a home, or a pattern of speech can bring back a flood of memories of the unequivocal warmth of a well-loved grandparent.

The power of this relationship is so universal that grandparents are the heroes in some of our best-loved

---

$\mathcal{T}$IP: Practice grandparenting on neighborhood children if you are separated by great distances from blood kin. The relationship will strengthen grandparenting muscles and add a missing warmth to your hearth.

---

children's stories and tales. In *Heidi*, for example, the child's grouchy grandfather showed her a whole new way of living. He fought like a tiger to maintain their bond when the outside world threatened to sever it. His grandchild offered him a return to the fullness of life as he saw the world around him renewed in her wonder and discovery. Fairy godmothers (grandparents in disguise) make a habit of showing up in the nick of time to create a ball gown, protect through a sleeping spell, or level the playing field in some essential way for their godchildren.

Everybody yearns for a grandparent with that magic touch. We reach out for that grandparent in our family. If we cannot find one there, we search elsewhere until we find that wise adult companion. Or we give up the search and vow to answer that need when our turn comes.

$\mathcal{T}$IP: Rent the video of *Heidi,* pop up some corn, and watch it with the grands.

❧ "My grandmother was always mad about something . . . perpetually cranky. We all stayed out of her way as much as we could. But there was this older woman on our corner that I could always go to. I knew she cared about me and that I could visit anytime. I went to her house and whispered all about my first loves, my hopes, my worries. I even learned to bake bread from her. I never smell hot, fresh bread without thinking about her. I guess she was my real grandmother."

—Jennifer, age 34

Our generation of grandparents can enjoy to the fullest each and every day we spend with our grandchildren. Our sense of adventure and discovery never needs to dim. We are healthier and heartier than any grandparents before us. We have more time, more energy, and the enthusiasm to seek new horizons and enlarge our new role in the family. With perfect timing, Mother Nature gives us the power to create magic when we are free enough and sufficiently fine-tuned to wave our wand expertly.

❧ "My grandmother was big and soft and comfortable. She always smelled like baby powder. She would read to me and I loved it, because she held me and put so much expression in her voice . . . Funny, I never thought of her as fat, just real full of good."

—Barb, age 46

something that you've only dared fantasize
ke up kayaking, zen gardening, boatbuild-
g, backpacking. Share your new passion with your
grands. Exercising creativity, passion, and rejuvena-
tion is just the right tone-up for grandparenting.

Tired of the family's perception of you? This is your
chance to transform yourself, to be reinvented in the eyes
of a brand-new human being. With this grandchild you
can explore areas you never had the time to reach before.
You can exchange your old practical image for a backpack,
because this grandchild is ready for adventure. Take up a
smock and brush, this grandchild will explore the arts
with you. Nostalgic for a baseball game with hot dogs and
peanuts? This grandchild is ready to go. You can leave
your true legacy with this grandchild and become a folk
hero in your family now and in the future. This is as close
as you will ever come to writing your own legend.

As grandparents, we have the priceless opportunity to
meld the past, present, and future in a continuous pattern
of growth for our family. We can ensure that the roots of
our family are strong enough to resist the erosion of values,
heritage, and self-worth.

ò "Grandparents are just very special people. My
grandparents had a tremendous influence on my
life. All of the things that I live by were things

they taught me. They were always spitting out these pearls of wisdom around the house. But they were things that my grandparents lived by and you learned the meaning of the words from their lives. I dedicated my doctoral dissertation to my grandfather, Daniel Webster Cooper. It was the biggest tribute I could pay him. He taught me what I really live by: if it's worth doing, it's worth doing right."

—Joyce, age 50

Grandparenting is unlike any experience life has offered before. It is like a day at the beach without sunburn, a picnic without ants, or income without taxation. Grandparenting is a job that we can tailor to our own specific style and talents. It has only one specific requirement. We have to care enough about our grandchild to want to share ourself with him.

On-again, off-again relationships cultivated only at holidays with no nurturing in between have little or no potential for magic. Our own best friends are the ones with whom we have shared all of ourselves—our hopes,

---

TIP: Create quiet moments together where a relationship can flower—a walk in the woods, breakfast out on Saturday mornings, a picnic in the snow, a few days together at the family weekend retreat.

dreams, experiences, great times, and awful times. If we allow our grandchildren to become merely acquaintances, we are passing up one of life's greatest rewards.

With our grandchildren we can share without nagging to achieve, love without having to instruct, play without teaching, comfort without having to assign blame. We can be so free that we can give this child all the things we could not fully give to our own children. Mother Nature set it up that way.

Let's take a great leap forward and elevate ourselves from parent to *grand*parent. Two o'clock feedings, potty training, table manners—gone! *Sayonara* to rule making, curfews, and "eat your peas." While Mom is striving for five food groups, Grandma can serve ice cream sundaes and eclairs for lunch (occasionally). Dad's fighting with algebra, but Gramps gets to take in a movie. We have the luxury of spending time with our grandchild because we enjoy her company.

No matter how seriously and lovingly we undertook our parenting role, we still had to juggle all the necessities of life. Our time was split between trying to put a roof over their heads, put food on the table, and pay attention to our careers. When we were finally alone with our

---

*T*IP: *Webster's New World Dictionary* defines *grand* as splendid, complete, most important, excellent. Go for it!

TIP: Keep a journal of thoughts, memories, and hopes while waiting for the birth of a grandchild. Continue this journal as the child grows.

---

children, we had to instill discipline, teach responsibility, round out their education, and, through it all, give each of them the love they needed. Grandparenting is not a repeat of parenting. It is a whole new role in life.

As we await the birth of our grandchild, our new role in the family should also grow and develop. Getting ready for grandparenting is entirely different from getting ready for parenting. There's no morning sickness or swollen feet, but there are changes. Our place in the family circle shifts, and subtle developments in our thoughts and attitudes are necessary to give birth to the grandparent in each of us.

It is time to recognize the adult status of our children. This time of preparation involves loving them as much as ever but also includes letting go. At long last, our children are all grown up. They have families of their own, and they must be allowed to take over the reins of their lives, their families, and their futures. We must allow our children the freedom to choose their own style, to make mistakes and learn from them. Offer help when requested, support without interference, and encouragement without criticism. Do everything possible to contribute to a family in harmony.

Most of us learned about family and parenthood in the

trenches. We had no choice but to wing it and try to do our best. All of us made mistakes. We bought books on parenting and asked other parents who seemed more successful for tips. What we wanted least of all was someone we loved looking over our shoulder and telling us what we should have done.

There really is no perfect way to raise children. All parents differ from one another and from their own parents as do all children. We don't have authoritative "cookbooks" to tell us the one true way to teach our children how to be responsible, cut their meat, use the toilet, be compassionate, master fractions, drive sanely, and choose the "right" kind of friends. We must allow our adult children to guide their families on the course they have chosen, using their own compass. Perhaps we did things differently, but they are not compelled by love or familial reverence to repeat exactly our parenting pattern.

✒ "My parents raised three daughters and to hear them tell it, we were all very well behaved. When my son arrived, they were thrilled. We drove the eight hundred miles several times a year for visits. I guess it was like culture shock for them to see their grandson so mobile, noisy, and inquisitive. Behaviors that I thought were normal worried them. I felt that they were disapproving or critical. It was very hard for all of us. Our visits were not comfortable; they were nerveracking. As the kids got older and more civilized, it got easier, but those early years were really hard."

—Kathy, age 49

Although fundamental family values do not change, the institution of family is not static. In order to be healthy, it must grow and adapt. The environment and culture in which our children raise their children differ from our own. Some of those changes are a natural evolution.

Our family circle may have already changed with the addition of a daughter or son-in-law. These new family members bring with them a heritage and tradition that will blend with our own within this new family unit. This is the time to become better acquainted with our "grand-in-laws." They are part of the extended family that we will share with this grandchild. Each of us is entitled to develop a relationship with our grandchild that is uniquely ours. But a respectful appreciation of the perspective that each of us brings to our blended family line will provide a harmonious world for our new grandchild.

---

*T*IP: When the desire for control asserts itself, repeat before a mirror, "They are all grown up! I've been promoted! I am a *grand*parent!"

‎‎ "We had a big extended family, all in the same city. Nana was the boss. Everyone loved her and respected her, and her word was the law in the family. I don't remember anyone resenting her, so she must not have meddled. She was more like a peacemaker who told others when to quit their foolishness and how to get along with one another. Everyone looked up to her. She had a great deal of power, but I only remember her using it for the good of the family."

—Joe, age 55

As important as the grandparenting relationship has been in the past, it is crucial in contemporary family life. Changes in the fundamental structure and function of our families occurred over the course of the last generation that require a greater degree of involvement from extended family members in our children's lives. Today's children face challenges that will make their childhood experiences entirely different from those of the generation before them. The American family is reconfiguring itself. The cost of being middle class has skyrocketed, and in many instances families can survive only through two

---

*T*IP: Pick up the phone and brag together with your grand-in-laws over the wonderful grandchild you share.

incomes. Full-time careers for many women have become not only an economic but a psychological necessity. Women do not want to confront an empty nest and an empty briefcase at the same time.

In the face of flux, the modern family rushes to cover all the bases. Our grandchildren will spend more of their time in structured activities during their day than any previous generation. They go to school, then to day care or structured lessons, play in sports leagues, belong to the Scouts, and hold jobs. They have very little free time to play Kick the Can with the neighborhood pack, climb a tree, or count lightning bugs at night. They are growing up in pinstriped suits and backpacks.

The odds are extremely high that our grandchildren will confront a shortage of time with parents who are both working to maintain the family income. Many children come home to empty houses. There's a fifty–fifty chance that their parents will separate or divorce. Schools, regardless of location, may not be able to maintain a peaceful environment. Too many will experience violence on their streets.

TIP: Ozzie and Harriet were a figment of our collective wishful thinking. We need a new vision of family dynamics that allows everyone to play with the cards they are dealt.

*T*IP: Get to know the caregivers in your grandchild's life. Drop by the day care center or offer to volunteer in a grand's school, club, or team activities.

Childhood in our contemporary society is a time of stress and worry. And for some children, childhood has all but disappeared. The reality that will not change significantly is that most parents will work outside the home. Other people will play an increasingly significant role in raising our grandchildren or they will have to raise themselves. Grandparenting offers children a powerful relationship in a noncompetitive, accepting atmosphere that will allow them to savor some of the most important aspects of childhood.

We come to our grandchild with all the bonds of blood and heritage and all the freedom of time and maturity. And we can have such fun together.

"I remember Pop used to take out his false teeth. He would hold them in his hand so his thumb and forefinger made a face around the teeth. He would draw a couple of eyes in pen on his forefinger and then his teeth would 'talk' to us. We thought it was hilarious. We'd beg him to make his teeth 'talk' when we came to visit. He never seemed embarrassed by it. I was surprised when my father

told me that Pop never wanted anyone to know
he had false teeth."

—Kate, age 32

Whether a first-time grandparent or an eighth-time
grandparent, whether we live next door or across the
continent from our grandchildren, we have a unique opportunity to do something wonderful both for ourselves
and each grandchild that is presented to us. We can bring
the heritage of the past to bear on the present and change
the future for our family and for the larger society. Grandparenting completes the family function of creating whole
and healthy individuals imbued with the best of the past
and full of hope for the creation of the future.

Modern grandparenting is waiting to be discovered by
a whole new generation. Grandparenting is a job that
develops vision, a sense of humor, commitment, and joy. It
is to be savored, to be enjoyed, and to be relished. It is the
best-paying job we will ever have.

2

Follow the Yellow Brick Road

❖

Grandparenting Offers a Brand-New Adventure

As grandparents traveling through life, we've gone places, done things, and lived. Maybe we've even taken our world a bit for granted. We're due for another trip down the yellow brick road. Now we have the opportunity to discover it once again in all its wonder through new eyes—those of our grandchildren.

Grandparenting is always an adventure! We'll find that each of our grandchildren is different—shy, self-assured, artistic, athletic, or cerebral—but what all children have in common are creativity and the spirit of discovery. As grandparents, we delight in the unique personality of each of our grandchildren. Together, we can traverse that very special grandparenting landscape where the practical and the mundane don't exist—or if they do, they give way to a special magical quality.

Children are born with a fascination for the world around them. As they grow, they need to know more about everything they encounter. Our grandchildren's sense of exploration and adventure is different from that of the adults around them. They explore for the joy of discovery, not to conquer a task or develop a product. As their world expands, we can find them sampling dustball hors d'oeuvres, trailing a busy caterpillar, or discovering what's making that noise inside the radio. They are free, uninhibited, and fascinated with finding out what makes things work.

Their logic is flawless. They are filled with colorful and enchanting explanations for what makes clouds and rainbows and fireflies. The magic of their world is contagious—cherish it. Mutual discovery and natural exploration work magic on the grandparent-grandchild relationship.

✍ "My granddaughter, Michelle, was nearly three the year the seventeen-year locust returned. I was about to go around the bend listening to their

---

TIP: Kids are born with a funny bone. Share some silly stuff with them. They are a great audience. Put on a wig and become a daffy character for a few moments, share chicken jokes, or visit a joke or magic store together.

cacophony and crunching them every time I took a step. The summer seemed like it would never end. Then Michelle came to visit. From the time she awoke each morning until the time she fell into bed each night, we collected the gosh darn critters. We took long walks together and filled her little bucket with all of the strange-looking bugs we could find. Then we brought them home, and she would spread them out and sort them into piles of those with one wing, those with sad eyes, fast ones, slow ones, dead ones, big ones, little ones. There were thousands of them. She gave them names and made up stories about them. Soon I stopped hearing the noise and was as excited as she was every time we found an interesting locust. She stayed for a week and neither of us grew tired of this activity. We still talk about the locusts a lot. They'll be back in a few years. We're both looking forward to it."

—Anthony, age 67

This open embracing of the world through exploration begins to diminish as the boundaries of our grandchildren's culture close in. Creative play experiences become increasingly rare. Instead of exploring with enthusiasm, they are expected to behave in a certain way, master writing a specific group of letters in a precise manner, and come up with the "right" answers when asked. Activities undertaken for pure enjoyment give way to activities that meet a goal or requirement. Grandparents can use their wizardry to extend that period of discovery by engaging in activities with their grandchildren that don't have a product or a lesson or an achievement tied to them—going jogging, fishing, bike riding, or tinkering with machinery. We have the luxury to explore and discover with our grandchildren through companionable activities and sharing of experiences. The way we spend our time together will determine the strength of the bonds we forge.

It really doesn't matter whether we have one hour, one afternoon, one weekend, or more to spend with our grandchildren—all time can be meaningful. Unlike adults, children tend to live in the present with all its potential for joy, adventure, and companionship. To the child, this minute matters above all others. The most dreaded words a young child hears from an adult are "just a minute."

As adults, we worry a great deal about time and how it can be saved, how it can be lost, how it can be wasted. We've become great time managers. Grandparents don't

---

TIP: Network with other grandparents. Squeeze in some factual exchange between the bragging. Ask about the interests of their grandchildren and successful activities they have shared. Modify these tips to fit your own family circle.

need to manage time with their grandchildren because we are usually not involved in their daily routine—catching the school bus or getting to the baby-sitter's on time. We can choose when and where we will spend time on our grandparent-grandchild quest. We can make each moment meaningful and value each minute of grandparenting time.

✍ "My husband and I were visiting my daughter and her family. The adults were chatting and my fifteen-month-old granddaughter was playing quietly at our feet. Suddenly aware of the music that was playing, Piper came over to my husband with outstretched arms and softly said, "Pa-pa." Joe immediately rose, whisked her into his arms, and started a funny little dance. They swirled and dipped, laughed and clapped, and gazed fondly into each other's eyes, genuinely enjoying the activity together. When the music ended, he gently plopped her back on the floor where she happily returned to her play."

—Charlotte, age 53

It's worth the effort to learn your grandchild's interests. How do they mesh with your own? If he's interested in dinosaurs, why not read up on dinosaurs? You might also find the topic fascinating. What is his favorite color, flavor, animal, place, activity? You can learn all of these things during the time that you spend with your grand-child. When a few minutes of grandparenting time present themselves through an unexpected visit or your grandchild answering the phone when you call your son or daughter, use them to explore this new personality.

⚘ "My grandfather didn't have any hobbies that I remember, but he used to do these weird, funny things with me. Once, we made a corral for ants out of piles of stones. We put bread crumbs on the top of the wall and then we watched the ants climb up, eat, and carry off the leftovers. I don't know how long that took. We just waited and watched together, slow and easy. He was a corporate lawyer, full of power and hustle at work, but I never felt him rushing around me."
—Fred, age 37

From the very first moment you hold your new grand-baby, you begin to discover the world anew. Instead of holding your granddaughter close to your chest, turn her around with her back to your chest and let her see the world go by. As you walk with her, let her explore the

---

TIP: Start conversations with your grandchild by asking her to tell you the silliest or most outrageous thing that happened to her this week.

textures of walls, bricks, silky curtains, bumpy picture frames—all these things are brand-new and fascinating. When Grampa holds his new grandbaby on his chest, he can hum in a low baritone. Not only will the sound fascinate her, it marks the beginning of your lifelong conversation.

Your toddler grandchild is a bundle of energy and curiosity. A simple trip to the park or the library can become a great adventure. He's into copying and modeling at this stage, so a child-sized rake or broom is a good investment, especially if you spend a few minutes working together. He'll really enjoy exploring potential personas at this age. Engage his imagination by giving him an old briefcase or purse. Let your lifestyle be your guide. Whatever you do for a living, provide some accoutrements of your trade for your grandchild. Or while taking a leisurely walk, gather interesting rocks, weeds, bottle caps, and feathers. It doesn't matter if at the end of your walk you're only half a block from home.

Create a treasure box for rainy days or quiet time. Find an old box or trunk, unique enough to capture a young child's imagination. Fill the box with creativity boosters: old jewelry, clothes, puzzles, magnifying glass, calculator, magnets, bubble blowers, empty cigar boxes. Periodically add a few new items for variety. Let your grandchild know that this is her special box, and then let her have plenty of time to explore the possibilities when she's visiting your home.

When the time comes for a rest, curl up together with a good book and some milk and cookies. Tell stories to each other, or look at a photo album. Your young grandchild will love to hear stories about you or his parents at his age. Flex those imagination muscles with some simple word games like "What if we had hair on our feet instead of our head? Why, we'd wear barrettes on our toes. We'd have to go to the barber for foot cuts." Try making up silly rhymes. Spread out a blanket in the backyard and stare up at the sky. Find animals and shapes in the clouds, or go out at night and wait and hope for shooting stars.

✍ "When I was real little, I'd sit on PapPap's lap in a rocking chair on the front porch of my grandparents' farm. He would tell me stories about the wild animals that lived in the woods around them. All those animals had a personal relationship with PapPap. The fox, for instance, over time got to know old PapPap and he brought his vixen to visit, but he knew better than to mess with PapPap's chickens. I used to beg him for one more story. When I took my own kids down to visit

---

TIP: Put on some music and dance with your grandchild.

him, I could hear him on the front porch telling those very same stories and my kids begging for just one more."

—Annie, age 50

As our grandchildren grow and enter school, their horizons explode beyond the boundaries of their secure family to include new friends and other families, as well as the downside: competition, evaluation, bureaucracy. Suddenly they must live according to a different set of rules for each activity in which they participate. Instead of being rewarded for their individuality, they are expected to behave in a certain way. Their time for discovery becomes severely limited as they begin to struggle with required conformity.

"I remember Grandad's workshop. It smelled like wood chips and lacquer. He had rows of coffee cans filled with nuts, bolts, screws, all kinds of stuff. When I went there, he would give me some scraps of wood and say, 'Tommy, my boy, let's see what you can do.' I had the freedom to use any of his things . . . I spent so many great hours fooling around in that shop with him. To me, it was like a castle, a dream come true. It was the perfect place . . . I could never understand when Grandma called it an eyesore. I really loved being in there, just the two of us."

—Tom, age 31

You don't have to dig up all new activities to share with your grandchild. You can enjoy your own interests and include her in them. If she shares your interests, plan an easy project together. If you like woodworking, try building a pair of stilts together. If needlework's the ticket, start a simple project in which you can both take part. Share your love of exercise by including her in a morning jog or an afternoon at the gym.

Remember that your grandchild may not be physically adept and may need a lot of encouragement. If the activity becomes frustrating, cut your losses and try something else later. Keep your project simple and fun. Perfection is not the goal here. The important part was the adventure you've shared and the memory that lives on in the wobbly stilts, rumpled needlework, or jogging habit. These are the precious mementos of the grandparenting journey.

✍ "I really love to do projects with my grandmother. She never goes and 'redoes' my work. We also never argue about how to do a thing. We just talk about it."

—Jamie, age 11

The opportunities for activities together expand as your grandchild's skills and understanding also expand. However, as your grandchild enters the preteen years, the going may not be so easy. Preteens are moody and opinionated, and they are subject to mood swings. Enthusiasm for your shared activity may wane a bit. If the treasured activity elicits zero interest, scrap it. Let flexibility be your guide as to whether you reschedule the same activity or plan a different one.

✍ "The boy had come to stay for the summer while his mother convalesced from a serious illness. He was not altogether thrilled with the arrangement. The first week was difficult. Then one morning, his grandfather told him that some animal was prowling in the garden at night. They needed to make a trap. The boy's interest was sparked a bit, and they built a contraption to catch the intruder. They set bait—a doughnut—to lure it in. The next morning, the bait was gone, the trap empty, and an unidentifiable track led away from the trap. A clue!

So began a ritual of reconfiguring the trap, trying different baits, and analyzing clues left behind. The process captured the boy's imagination and enthusiasm. The summer passed, and they never caught the animal. It was, they decided together, a sly old fox. I was that boy."

—Tony, age 33

As your grandchild nears adolescence, he is starting to look at time the same way you are. He has precious little of it and he may not be as willing to share that free time with you. He may not be as eager to go places, preferring to hang around the house on the off chance that a friend will call.

This is the time to listen, listen, listen, *without* giving unasked-for advice or judgment. Work at being the best, and maybe the only, nonjudgmental adult in this older child's life. This is the time to expand your world to include hers. Ignore the hairstyle, lipstick, nail polish, earrings, clothing, or music. Each generation has its own unique look while finding its way to adulthood. Share your own silliness with your grand. See what she thinks of Nehru suits, pillbox hats, and bell-bottoms. Ask her opinions on current events, social activities, or movies. Listen carefully to her opinions and vow to discuss them nonjudgmentally.

"Gramma is so cool. She let me paint her toenails black and she kept it on. Mom freaked out when she saw Gramma's toes."

—Nora, age 15

Give him the opportunity to begin doing adult things with you and for you. Ask him to record a message for your

---

TIP: Adolescents strapped for time are still just a phone call away. A five-minute phone call to touch base with them strengthens the link between generations.

answering machine and leave it on so he can call and hear it himself. Ask his opinion on clothing selections, hairstyles, stereo equipment, music groups. Then try it out. If he is computer literate and you are struggling to get onto the information highway, ask him to help you out. Subscribe to magazines that suit his growing interest: car magazines, teen magazines, music magazines. Let him choose movies for you to watch together.

❧ "I was the only boy, and while Gram did things with the girls, Pap always found some special thing for me to do with him. I remember this one time when I was about twelve. He had an old toilet in the garage. We put drop cloths over it and under it. Then he gave me a sledgehammer. He gave it to me, and he just smiled this kind of sly smile. I couldn't believe it. He wanted me to smash it. He never said one word, just smiled and nodded at that old toilet. It took a while, but finally I hit it. Too gently. Nothing happened. He

---

*T*IP: Respect and utilize the developing abilities of grandchildren. Being chosen to do a real-world job recognizes competence. Ask them to design some personal letterhead for you, plan the menu for the next family gathering, return a purchase, pick out your present for their parent's birthday.

smiled more broadly, and I whacked it a good one, and it started to give. Again and again I smashed it. I can still hear it breaking over the sound of Pap laughing. His old voice and my young one, ringing with laughter."

—Paul, age 26

As a group, teenagers receive a great deal of intolerant attention from their elders. Although almost grown, they refuse to dress and talk like adults. They know they have a very small window of time left before they must play by society's rules and they take full advantage. Just remember that underneath the outrageous clothing and unique hairstyle is the same grandchild you have loved and praised since birth.

Just as most grandparents have more time to spend, teens have less. Between school, job, sports, college prep courses, romance or lack thereof, and friends, time is pinched and precious. Grandparents need to make the most of short spurts of contact, just as parents do. The trick in doing things with teens involves including their friends or planning for a time when peers won't be missed,

---

TIP: Teenage grandchildren have *not* outgrown the need for grandparental approval. Say as often as you can, "I'm so impressed that you . . ." and utilize the moment.

capitalizing on the natural events in a teen's life, finding situations where they can show off their muscle or their competence, and supporting their efforts to define themselves as they move into the adult world.

 "My grandparents always had their grandchildren come each year to string popcorn for an outdoor Christmas tree for the birds. We ate more than we strung and more than once got into a contest to see how much thrown popcorn we could catch with our mouths. As I remember it, we were pretty wild with that popcorn. It was too cold to do it outdoors, so we worked and played in the big kitchen. I thought about those times when I had children and a home of my own. I once asked Nana why she never told us to cut it out. 'No reason,' she said. 'You were just kids doing what came naturally. When you were finished, I'd give you a broom and a bag and you would clean it all up for the birds.' Funny, I don't remember that part at all."

—Paula, age 39

Teens are always short of money. Contract with your teenage grandchildren to paint a room in your house, clean out your basement, or do a landscape job. Pay them when the job is finished according to the going rate, and schedule it so they have enough time to do the job.

We are sharing a journey of discovery with our grand-children. As we travel down the road, we have much to learn about each other and our world together. Our adventures will sometimes succeed beyond our wildest dreams and other times fall miserably short. But most importantly, we will have shared and learned and loved together. We have forged a special bond that will endure forever.

3

Mirror, Mirror on the Wall

❖

Reflecting the Best
in Our Grandchildren

Criticism is easy to get. People will line up cheerfully anytime to count our warts for us. No wonder Snow White's mean old stepmother hung a mirror compelled to flatter. What she really needed was a caring grandparent who loved her, warts and all, to hold up a mirror reflecting a worthwhile human being in the making. With that kind of support, Snow White would have had a far better childhood and a terrifying villainess would be missing from our fairy tales.

Hand in hand, we have explored the world with our grandchildren, giving them space and time to experience the wonder of personal discovery. Our grandchildren also need to believe that every single one of us has worth and value. Each of us has important contributions to make to

*T*IP: If you are handy with a needle, make your grandchild a baby quilt or a soft toy. If not, commission someone who is. Send one to each grandchild.

---

the world around us. We have skills to give, and we also have values to live by. Expecting the schools and groups in which our children spend more and more of their time to do the whole job of promoting individual self-worth and nurturing human virtues is a pipe dream at best and a sign of indifference at worst.

From the moment they are born, children are the subject of comparisons among siblings, peers, teammates, and schoolmates. These comparisons greatly influence a child's sense of self-worth. Even now, as adults, when others tally us up and find us wanting, it hurts. Within a family, no matter how loving and enlightened, birth order, size, or maturity dictate what a particular child's rights, privileges, and responsibilities will be in the family structure.

Because grandparents can choose to focus their attention in a different way, they, above all family members, can reflect a positive sense of personal value to a grandchild. The "grand" attitude in essence is: "You are so wonderful that there are no conditions, no strings, no ifs. Simply because you are my grandchild, you are wonderful."

✍♥ "When I was a little girl and we went to see Daddy Preacher, he would always be waiting for us sitting on the rocker on the front porch of their old farmhouse. When I would get out of the car, he'd throw his arms wide and say, 'It's my little princess!' I'd run into his arms. It made me feel so special, and I kept that feeling as I grew up. Even when I was married and brought my kids back to see him (gosh, he must have been a hundred years old then), he still said to me, 'Well if it isn't my little princess!' "

—Joleen, age 57

Your grandchild is likely to be experiencing less and less one-on-one time with his parents than you did as a child with yours. Out of necessity, the modern parent is burning the candle at both ends and must opt for "quality time." Grandparents willing to lavish a whole afternoon or weekend on one grandchild not only allow this grandchild to bask in much-needed attention but give their adult children an unexpected breather. You don't need a hundred and one trombones and crashing cymbals each and every time you entertain your grandchild. Children relish undivided attention and companionship. It is during this kinder, simpler time together that you may reveal yourself to those you trust.

"My grandmother takes me to the movies. It's so special to me because we go without all my other sisters. She's my movie friend."

—Ramona, age 8

Concentrate on valuing the uniqueness of your grand-child during your time together. Strengthening good character traits or mending behavior is always accomplished better with stealth. Catch her in the act of doing good and praise her. Otherwise, this is what you could end up with:

☙ "All she ever wants to do is clean my room and run everyone's life. I wish she'd get a life of her own and butt out of mine."

—Kyle, age 16

Begin immediately to let your grandchild know how unique and how wonderful his approach to the world is. Even babies know you find them enchanting if you get down on the floor with them. Throw your dignity to the wind—you want this grandchild to know from the very start that he is so special that he can have your total attention whenever he needs it.

☙ "Pop-pop died when I was very young. My memories are hazy, but mostly I remember that he always got down on the floor with me. I don't remember what we did, but I know that he made

---

TIP: Focus on special characteristics that you see in your grandchildren. Stroke them every chance you get.

me feel very special, very important . . . I really wish I could have known him longer."

—Juliet, age 24

Toddlers seem to be everywhere at once, getting into some form of mischief. Take their energy and run with it. Showing how much you value their help can make you a hero in their eyes. An adult who really wants their help is the answer to their prayers. Including your grandchildren in the real tasks that you do and praising their work is a marvelous way to instill the idea that they can do a good job. You need to break the jobs down beforehand into their very simplest steps and work slowly along with them. Emphasize the fun in a job. Washing the car can be a lot of fun if you can get really wet doing it.

"My grandfather would ask me to shave with him when I was just a little boy. I would stand on the toilet seat so we could both see ourselves in the mirror. We would make a big production of lathering up with shaving cream and then shave it off together. Of course, my razor had no blade. Sometimes he would decide that we needed a second or even a third shave. He was a surgeon and a very busy man. I don't know how he found the time for me, but he always did. I still love the smell of Barbasol, and I never use an electric razor."

—Tommy, age 38

Mastery of the world around us should begin as early as possible. Your preschool grandchild loves words. She is an insatiable information hound. Help her develop practical skills to get what she needs. Learning to use the telephone, the library, the computer, the fax machine, and the copier, as well as paying and getting change at the candy counter, makes any child feel that she can learn and do. Let your grandchild begin to understand that she can make changes and has the power to affect the world around her.

Present a problem to this grandchild and ask his help in solving it. "You have good ideas. What do you think we should do?" These problems are small when our grandchild is small and get bigger as his world grows. Ask the grandtoddler to decide which color dinner napkins should grace the table, and go with it even if the color scheme makes your eyes water. Ask this preschool grandchild who is bursting with ideas to help arrange the cans on the pantry shelf. Tell him you haven't been able to figure out

---

*T*IP: Add a homemade smock to your grandchild's wardrobe. This can be simply a large old shirt that you button up the back. It will lessen your worries about keeping your grandchild's come-to-visit clothes presentable when he is returned to his parents.

where the small cans should go. Can he help you? Then do it according to his scheme. Gather your grandchild into your lap and tell him stories in which the main character shares his name. Make your grandchild's namesake the hero of the story, who solves all the problems and brings order to the world. Don't make these stories too elaborate because you will have to repeat them many times.

℘ "Oh, I had a wonderful grandmother. I have so many memories of doing things with her when I was growing up. She had these 'secret' recipes for cake frosting. Nobody else's was as good as hers. When she was making a cake, we'd go into the kitchen and she'd say, 'This is my secret recipe.' She'd put her fingers to her lips and we'd talk real quiet. I was the only one she ever told that recipe to. It's still our secret."

—Debbie, age 27

As our grandchildren grow and pass through school, they have an even greater need to define themselves without competition and judgment. Be there, unchanged and

---

𝒯IP: Save oversized boxes to use as blocks for building a skyscraper, play house, fort, or other construction.

continually supportive. That is our role. They don't have to win a ribbon for us. Grandparents can really help through this period because we know

- the smartest person is not always the best;
- it takes all kinds to make the world spin;
- at age 12, most of us had no idea that we would wind up where we did, doing what we do.

Armed with a feeling of self-worth, our grandchildren can begin to stretch and exercise their particular capabilities. Problem solving, utilizing their own unique capabilities and perceptions, allows them to plumb the unique person within them. Grandparents can subtly reinforce this process.

When a gorgeous sunset presents itself, stop to watch and wonder. When construction projects are underway in your neighborhood, walk down to view the progress. When a neighbor is sick, prepare some cookies or soup

---

TIP: Write a story together in ongoing installments. When words dry up, illustrate the finished pages. Research the bindery process at the library, and bind the book. When it is finished, present it to your grandchild's parents or keep it yourself, display it prominently, and read it to younger grandchildren.

and together take it to them. Pausing for beauty, stopping to watch skillful work, and helping out those around you are all ways that you can slow down your grandchildren's pace and allow them to see that there are alternatives, potentials, and immutable truths in everyday life.

Through observation and action, our grandchildren learn the virtues that express the best in us and make us truly human—patience, empathy, tolerance, industry, honesty, tact. Those attributes that we reinforce in our grandchildren will grow and flourish. Since nearly all of the other forces in our culture support power, achievement, and complexity, we can counterbalance those limited values with more positive ones. Grandparents can choose to intensify those personal traits in their grandchildren that reflect humanism. And in that way, child by child, family by family, the world may become a more caring, loving, and pleasant place to live.

"Hazel was the greatest. She practically raised me. One of the most important things I learned from her was tolerance. I never heard her say an unkind word about anyone. Not ever. It wasn't from weakness either; it was from strength. She could talk to anyone because she respected everyone. I remember she took me to every church in our little southern town, even a synagogue."

—Jody, age 51

Many of us were nurtured in a more personal society. We knew our neighbors. Those of us who grew up in the Depression could put a personal face on poverty. Later generations grew up helping the elderly and less fortunate before our neighborhoods changed to bedroom communities. We gave to real people, not just organizations. We learned from dexterous neighbors how to tinker with cars. We provided entertainment for ourselves through picnics, parades, or family reunions. Now we have the United Way, planned obsolescence, and TV. Maybe these things represent progress, but if we lose the human connection, the impetus to share and laugh together is weakened.

When your grandchildren wonder aloud about some problem they perceive in society, that is your cue to help them explore it in a personal way. If they worry about the environment, begin to take simple direct action together: feed the birds, recycle, use only organic substances on your lawn. Tell your grandchildren that they made you see the problem and take that action. If they worry about poverty and inequality, help someone together.

✍ "Every Christmas Eve, Pop and I would go shopping for a warm coat. Then we'd go downtown

---

TIP: Sponsor a child together in another country. Jointly write letters to this child and share the commitment and discovery.

and drive around until we found some homeless guy. Pop would park the car and give me the coat, and I'd give that guy a brand-new warm coat. As I got older and had some money of my own, it got to be a tradition that I would put some of my money in the pocket."

—Toby, age 18

You can help your grandchildren learn the warmth of helping other people and strengthen the bonds between yourself and your grandchildren as well as the bonds between your grandchildren and their fellow human beings. Charity can truly begin at home when you help your grandchildren fix a sibling's broken bike or stitch up a sibling's overloved animal that is dribbling stuffing. When you help your neighbors out, include your grandchildren in the activity. Together you can take toys to a shelter for homeless families, join a group that takes sandwiches to the homeless, or donate some of your cast-off furniture to a needy family in your church.

When your grandchildren get older, they are often caught in a situation where learning, social life, or sports activities are not going smoothly. From time to time, all of us get the blues. When our rhythms are out of sync, we need to talk about what's bothering us. Hardly anyone really listens to children's thoughts, yet their ideas are valid. Don't moralize, just listen. If they ask for an opinion, try to give them the least judgmental answer possible.

You'll find sharing an incident from your own life, especially one where you were not a winner or hero, is a wonderful way to open a dialogue with your grandchildren.

Learning can also be hidden in play. When you have some quiet time with your grandchild, fool around with imaginary scenarios. For instance, ask questions: If you were lost in the woods on a rainy night, what would you do? If the roof started to leak, what would you do? What if you lost your voice and broke your right (or left, for lefties) hand, how would you communicate with people? What if you were the president or the principal, what are three things that you would do?

As your grandchild grows, she can find great satisfaction in learning to take care of herself. Enable her to develop practical skills, and she'll get the satisfaction of personal achievement. Show her the inside of the car engine, help her check the oil and water gauges, and show her how to use a tire gauge. If the air is low, go together to the gas station and show her how to fill the tires. Let her learn to be competent in the practical areas of her life.

✍ "My grandparents had a large farm. What I remember most was working with my grandad. He treated me like I was a man, like I was really important. He would say, 'Come on, Ronny, we got work to do.' We fixed fences, we planted corn and worked the cows. We did all kinds of things that never seemed like chores. I learned to like work from him. I learned to do all kinds of things that city kids never dreamed of. That old man was a genius to me, and he couldn't even read."

—Ron, age 65

Family get-togethers provide an opportunity to give your grandchild a real job. Working to make something happen creates an interested participant, not a bored observer. Ask your grandchild to take on the responsibility for preparing Jell-O for dessert. Give him the package and some extra ingredients and let him concoct whatever he wants. Praise his effort and ask him to do it the next time you get together. Even though you may get sick of Jell-O, you will never tire of his sense of achievement.

Prepare a simple one-dish meal together. Be sure to make enough so your grandchild can take dinner home for his family. His parents will love the free dinner! Or make microwave fudge together. Give him the recipe so he can cheer the family with fudge whenever the need arises. He

---

TIP: Thinking of redecorating? Hire your teenage grandchild as an assistant painter, paperhanger, or general gofer.

should know he can call you if he runs into trouble with the recipe.

Your responsibility is to show your grandchildren how to do a job and then let them do it. Trial and error is the best teacher. It takes patience and grit to master a skill. Let her design the setting for the dinner table—from dishes to flowers. Don't rearrange them when she is finished. King Fahd isn't coming to dinner tonight, so the protocol doesn't have to be perfect. Thank her and appreciate the difference from your own arrangements. Praise her work and tell her what you've learned from her.

🍃 "When she came for a visit, Gran always helped each of us kids make one family dinner. One year, when I was about 11, I remember going to the store, cooking, and serving a meal you wouldn't believe. Gran helped me make chicken and dumplings with gravy, mashed potatoes with gravy, buttered noodles with gravy, and, of course, biscuits in gravy. She must have clued my parents in beforehand, because no one commented on the enormous amount of starches and fats. I remember feeling very confident and successful. As I grew up, however, I sure took my share of teasing over that meal. On her birthday last year, I invited the family to my apartment and duplicated that masterpiece meal. She loved it."

—Merrily, age 23

If our grandchildren have the loving reflection of our eyes and our hearts, they will never need a magic mirror. From us will come the unequivocal knowledge that they are persons who are inherently valuable and innately worthwhile. Armed with the respect bestowed by a beloved elder, they can face down any obstacles as they grow toward their own future. They will succeed because they know and we know that they can.

4

Geppetto Loved His Boy

❖

Helping Grandchildren Feel Secure

Truant! Liar! Cheat! Those were the encouraging words the outside world hurled at Pinocchio. Jiminy Cricket all but washed his hands of the blockhead on several occasions, and the Blue Fairy's big gift was a reverse nose job. Geppetto, however, offered love, support, and belief in his beloved, magical boy. Bolstered by wise Geppetto's faith and encouragement, Pinocchio repaired his mistakes and became a good citizen.

Grandparents know that no one skates through life without making some mistakes. We made our share and we survived. Our life experiences give us a wide view that allows us to place life's problems into a proper perspective. What seems like Mount Everest to our children and our grandchildren assumes a more realistic proportion in our eyes. We know that all kids will be toilet trained before high school, we don't know too many thirty-year-olds who still wear their baseball hats backward, and we also know that not too many people use algebra after they stagger out of the classroom.

Grandparents can put trouble in a suitable frame and help everyone get the proper perspective. That is what has made us fairy godparents to generations of grandchildren.

✍❤ "My grandmother is a college professor and probably the smartest person I've ever met. Years ago, when I was flunking high school biology and my world was crumbling, she told me in secret that she failed biology in tenth grade. I think that was the best present she could have given me then."
—Amy, age 22

Just as we open a world of discovery for our grandchildren and cultivate the best parts of their natures, we need to be there to catch our grandkids when the sky is falling.

When children are very young, they tend to make many little mistakes. They quarrel, spill, fuss, and break things. Often their mistakes get more attention than their triumphs. These early years are the time to help children learn how to fix mistakes, make someone feel better, repair a broken cup or a cracked relationship. Mistakes have a positive learning side to them. If a glass is broken and

*T*IP: **When something is broken or a relationship is in tatters, help your grandchild write an "I'm sorry" note to the offended party.**

---

juice spilled, we can work together with our grand-children, in a supportive way, to clean it up. It is certainly not the first nor will it be the last spill.

Giving our grandchildren a hand in correcting their mistakes allows them to learn from errors and to move on to the relief of expiation and forgiveness. There are two very important things that our grandchildren need to learn about any mistakes that they make. First, they must work to make it right, and second, they must find ways to avoid doing the same thing again. Our grandchildren will hurt themselves, their parents, siblings, friends, pets, toys, flowers, walls, and carpeting in many different ways as they grow. Grandparents know that there are always things to be done to set it right.

✍ "I was about five and really coveted a spoon that my father had brought back to my mother from one of his trips. As I look back on it now, it was a tacky souvenir thing that he brought her just for laughs. She hung it in the kitchen, and my fingers itched to get at it. One day, I took it down and took it to my room. And I broke it. I hid the broken pieces in a dark corner under my bed. But I couldn't stop worrying about it. It got so I couldn't sleep at night. My gram came for a visit. We were sitting on the front porch in a glider. She had on a blue flowered dress. (How can I remember that!) Suddenly I just blurted out to her what I had done. I cried, and she comforted me and then she took me by the hand. 'Let's go fix it,' she said. We got the pieces out and some glue and put it back together. Then she took my hand, and we went and told my mother. I never felt such relief before or since."

—Nicole, age 27

Often, especially when our grandchildren are young, we can help them tape, glue, or scrub up their mistakes. Doing something positive to restore things helps our grandchildren see that they are good at repairs, that they can be constructive in the face of disaster. This positive action shrinks their errors and magnifies their powers of repair. Sometimes, however, the errors are permanent. And we must help them to deal with these as well.

☙ "When I was about ten, I threw a stick at a dove. I was just trying to see if I could hit something. I never dreamed I would. Well, somehow I hit it just right and killed it. I was so guilty. I ran home and told my folks. They talked with me and kept pointing out that it was an accident. But I just didn't feel any better. My grandfather was visiting. He asked me to show him the bird. Together we dug a grave and buried the bird. There was another dove that kept hanging around. Grandfather explained that was the dove's mate. He asked me if I would like to put up a bird feeder near the grave and maybe the dove's mate would feed there and be comforted. I kept that feeder full all year long."

—Michael, age 29

The sky seems to leak often once grandchildren enter school. The struggle for acceptance is continuous and feelings bruise easily. When our grandchildren are left out of the most popular kids' sleepover invitations, can't make the right soccer team, need braces, or are placed in the lower math group, life seems overwhelming. Grandparents can calmly help them understand that this too shall pass. Don't try to minimize the pain. It is very real.

As they move into their preteen years, children constantly weigh themselves against their peers and too often find themselves woefully wanting. Every preteen would jump at the chance to exchange his or her body and talents for another completely different set. Even the most physically gifted and talented feel this way. All of us can remember our own painful encounters with the all-

*T*IP: Sponsor an outing with your grandchild and two or three of his friends. Do the planning together, but let your grandchild play host. Take a background seat, but be ready to join in if needed or wanted.

---

powerful and incredibly cruel peer group or facing the irrefutable knowledge that we are not the best at something. But we also know that we survived it.

One of the greatest aspects of grandparenting is the ability to listen to our grandchildren's pain and problems and know that they are not unique. Many others before and since have struggled with the same problems and survived them. We know what worked for us, and we can try to help them find a solution that works for them.

✍ "Last year this group of really mean girls started picking on me. They would move away from me at the lunch table and whisper about me. They would make plans to do things in front of me and never ask me. I really felt bad. My grades got bad, too. My gramp knew about my problem, everybody did. One day he told me that he had three tickets to an ice show, one for him, one for me, and one for the newest girl at school. Janie had come to school two weeks before, and I didn't know her at all. I wanted to ask one of the mean girls. 'Nope,' said Gramp, 'they have each other. The new girl needs you.' Well we went and we had a great time. Janie and I are best friends now. Those other girls leave us alone. Gramps was so smart."

—Rachel, age 12

One aspect of growing up that our society sadly overlooks is the fact that doing something to the best of our ability is its own reward. Some competition can be good because it pushes us to go beyond what we thought we could do. But not everyone can be the best. The word would then have no meaning. Not winning the prize or ribbon may be a disappointment to our grandchildren. But by doing their very best, they have already achieved something of great value. Grandparents can reinforce the idea that satisfaction should come from doing our best— whether it is sweeping the walk, playing the piano, or running the mile. There is honor in knowing we've done a good job. Blue ribbons fade, but the personal satisfaction of knowing we've done the very best we can remains a part of each job we do. We can teach our grandchildren how to be their own best judge of achievement.

---

*T*IP: Designate a spot in your garden for your grandchild. Plant a pumpkin vine. Together, pinch off most of the blossoms and grow this year's killer jack-o'-lantern.

❧ "I love to swim, but I was frustrated that I wasn't placing in the swim meets. We had some really fast swimmers, and no matter how hard I tried, I just could not catch up with them.

"My grandfather started coming to my meets because my dad had to work. He watched my events and kept track of my times. Then one day he said, 'You know, Matt, your times are really improving.' He was right. I had shaved several seconds off of all of my times since the season had begun. Every time I swam, he was there cheering me on and my times got faster and faster. By the end of the season, I still had not come in first, but I had my best times ever."

—Matt, age 17

We may never be captains of industry, but without competent workers who take pride in their work, industry would not flourish. Most of us will not achieve greatness outside our family circle. But all of us can achieve great satisfaction from the work that we do and the lives that we live.

As adolescence rolls around, our grandchildren's potential for making mistakes takes a giant leap forward. Our grandteens are scared to death of having to grow up but insistent on the freedom to do so. The luckiest teenagers on earth are the ones who have caring grandparents waiting in the wings to listen to their troubles and point them in the right direction. A conversation overheard:

✍ "Nana, I really blew it this time."

"Tell me."

"I got a ticket for running a red light."

"That is serious."

"Mom and Dad are going to kill me."

"Probably not, although they may think about it."

"What am I going to do?"

"You are going to have to tell them, and you are going to have to take some heat."

"What are they going to do?"

"I don't know, but I do know some things that you can do."

"Like what?"

"Take full responsibility, no excuses, no defenses, a clean 'I did it, I feel very badly about it, I'll pay for it any way you say.' You know the words; you can handle this."

"It won't be easy."

"No, it won't be easy, but I know you can do it."

"I love you, Nana."

"I love you, too, and I'm very proud of you."

In past generations, lucky children who found things too tough to face at home could run away to Grandma and

Grandpa's house. Parents were grateful to know that their children were running from one safe harbor to another. All of us have the need for some space apart when we are wrestling with personal perspective and family relationships. If we have nurtured a bond with our grandchildren that is open and genuinely supportive, they will naturally turn to us in time of need. When they do, we have the priceless opportunity to stitch our family together a little tighter.

Often our grandchildren merely want to vent their frustration on ears that do not seem disloyal. This is the stance we must perfect. We must be willing to hear them out without criticism of *either* party and find the common ground in the middle where both sides can get together.

"There are four kids in our family, and when I was younger, I always felt that my parents loved my older sister more than me. I was very jealous of just about every thing she ever got to do.

One day, my grandfather held up my hand and asked me which of my fingers I loved the best. Of course, I couldn't choose. 'That's how it is with parents,' he said. For some reason, that made things clear up for me. I can't say that I've never felt jealous since, but when I do, my hand and Pop's words are always there to help."

—Priscilla, age 19

All normal, healthy teenagers try to manipulate the adults around them. This is actually a very good survival skill for living in the real world. Grandparents can see a con building from a mile away. After all, we've been on both sides of adolescence. Just remember never, under any circumstances, undermine a parent's position. Some open discussion with parents can help them remember that there are usually some bumps and bruises from shaky first flights. But in time, our grandchildren will soar.

🖎 "My daughter had been lobbying for jeans she didn't need and I couldn't afford. She called Gramma and tried to wheedle them out of her. Mom was never anybody's fool. She invited Jen to come over and help her do some housecleaning in return for the jeans. That way, I didn't look like a monster and Jen learned another way to get what she wanted."

—Phyllis, age 40

As our grandchildren near the point of departure, a host of family concerns bubbles to the surface. Will they get into good colleges? What will they do if they don't go to college? Can the family deal with plumbers or mechanics instead of doctors or lawyers? What possible good can come of traveling about the country with a backpack for a year? How can they consider getting married this young?

*T*IP: Write a letter from your heart to your grandchild. Tell her how much you value her as a person—her compassion, humor, generosity, and so on. Give no advice, simply let her know how important she is to you because of her own uniqueness.

✍ "I grew up in a port town where all the young guys went to work on the docks. It was a very tight community, and my family was at the center of it. I always wanted to be a doctor. My parents tried to talk me into the docks and tried to show me how impractical my ambition was given our financial circumstances. My grandmother always told me, 'Follow your dream.' She couldn't give me money or connections. But she gave me something more precious. She made me believe in myself when no one else did. She had another saying that I will always remember. 'Life's not easy, so you might as well make it interesting.' It was a long, hard haul, but I made it. Her faith kept me going until I made it."

—Eddie, age 43

Grandparents know that life goes on and that crises can be solved if good people keep their heads on straight. We have known people who were miserable failures as human beings although they held degrees from laudable institutions. We have known people who were incorrigible adolescents for fifteen years and then suddenly emerged like butterflies from a worn-out chrysalis into a beautiful adult life. We have known people who left and lost their families forever because no one understood their needs. Grandparents can provide the depth and breadth of wisdom that helps families find the point where love and support launch young people in the direction that they must go.

No experience is a waste. We can learn as much from our mistakes as we do from our successes, sometimes more. Because Geppetto could accept the blockhead years with Pinocchio and invest the love and compassion necessary, he became a real boy instead of a puppet. We do not want our grandchildren to be puppets waiting for someone else to pull their strings. We want them to realize their potentials and become real human beings. Many of us would never have planned and charted a course that brought us to exactly where we are now. Grandparents can call upon the wisdom of their own experience and past to shelter their grandchildren when the sky seems to be falling.

5

Wicked Stepmothers, Ogres, and Crones

❖

Finding the Best Role in a Changing Family

Over the generations we carefully stitch together the patchwork quilt of family. We are given no choice in the colors or patterns that life supplies. How well we blend these materials—harmoniously combining the somber and the gay, creatively assembling the weak and strong—determines how warm and serviceable that quilt will be when the outside world blows cold, harsh winds against our door.

Fairy tales are full of wicked stepmothers, mean old crones, or ogres that play one-dimensional roles and are banished from the hearth. In real life there are many dimensions to people and to happiness. Unfortunately, many of us are still looking for fairy-tale endings for our children, who are supposed to marry well and stay together. We don't want to envision any other scenario, but our modern society offers many variations on this theme.

As fully grown adults, we know that life is not simple. As a family we cannot totally avoid painful circumstances. In times of stress and pain, families need to develop the skill of creative problem solving. It helps no one to pore over the bad stuff and assign guilt. Roles assigned in the heat of the moment begin to take on a life of their own and are self-perpetuating. They add tension and insecurity to the lives of our grandchildren and thwart family harmony. We cannot shield our grandchildren from real pain in a family, but we can remain constant in our attitude toward them and in setting the tone to make the best of what we have. They will always and forever be our grandchildren, no matter what the circumstances of their specific family are. We are tied to them. If their family situation changes, we are still bound to them. Through this relationship, our family continues.

It is an unfortunate fact of modern life that fifty percent of marriages don't make it over the long haul. When families divide, grandparents need not be cut off from their grandchildren. Our grandchildren are not

---

TIP: Educate yourself about modern family issues. There are many good books on the subject that will help you understand the territory.

involved in the decision to split up a marriage, but they are very much involved in the consequences of the dissolution. It is part of our role in the family to provide constancy of affection, evenness of temper, and peace.

🌿 "Things stink at my house right now. My parents are all stressed out over the divorce. I go to my grandmother's to mellow out, you know, sleep and eat and stuff."

—Steve, age 17

It may help our grandparenting perspective to understand some of the dynamics involved in divorce or separation. Once we understand the patterns of behavior that are playing out before us, then we can develop strategies that will help us continue to play the role of Gran or Gramp rather than judge and jury.

When marriages falter, one or both partners know that something is going sour. But at the beginning, no one else is told about the problem. This phase can last for years as the partners make efforts in private to repair or restructure the marital bond. This is a time when questions from the

---

TIP: When families are in trouble, phone calls that begin "I was just thinking of you," and go on to cheerful subjects are the best received.

outside, even well-meaning ones, are abruptly brushed aside, often with anger. The need to protect the marriage in all its fragility takes priority over the need to confide and seek help. We've told our children over and over again that we "just want them to be happy" and "they should make their own choices." No wonder then, that when the biggest choice they made goes sour, they don't want us to know about it. And they are even more adamant about keeping their children from knowing that there is a threat of family fracture.

Our best strategy during this period is not to pry. Our children know that we care. If they could tell us, they would. But they can't really tell anyone right now. Our grandchildren probably don't know anything definite just now, although they probably suspect something is amiss. It is certainly not our place to question them. Wait to be told. Don't fish for information.

Children are emotional barometers for the family. When parents are not getting along, children sense it immediately and tend to feel that they are somehow responsible for the bad feelings in the home. A poor self-concept goes hand in hand with this realization. They seem to think, "My parents are tense and unhappy. They tell me that nothing is wrong. But I know I make lots of mistakes, so I probably did something to cause this, too."

Grandparents can help before these feelings get out of hand. Children need to know that adults both make and solve their own problems. They need to know that when parents argue, children should stay out of the way. They need to know that they are cherished for all of their human frailties as well as their strengths. And above all they need to know that there is peace and safety in the heart of their grandparents always.

✍ "I was 13 when Dad left us. I know that they weren't real happy, but I had no idea that he would just walk out on us. I got real mad at my mom, too. I felt ugly and mean all the time. My mom had all my problems and then all of hers, too. I started to cut school and drink. I was going down the tubes.

"Then my grandparents asked me to come on a cross-country trip with them, you know? I went, but I was really doing it to get away from Mom and all her yelling. But that trip was great. We, like, didn't have any real schedule, we just did stuff, like hike or shop or just look around. I kept track of what we spent and how much we had left, 'cause they said we could keep going while the money held out. We never talked about my problems, but we talked a lot about what I wanted to

---

*T*IP: Send a gift certificate to a favorite family restaurant to your grandchild and let him take the family out to dinner on you.

do and how I could do it, you know, going to college and stuff.

"When we came home, Mom looked a lot better and I guess I did, too. We mellowed out with each other. That trip with my grandparents was something I'll never forget."

—Nan, age 18

As the tension builds toward a breakup in a marriage, hostility becomes crystal clear. There are more public arguments, and the tension becomes impossible to hide. Children, parents, neighbors, and friends are aware that this marriage is crashing on the rocks. Everyone has well-intentioned advice to offer; everyone knows what should be done to shore up the marriage. However, the best and only advice is to see a professional who can be objective and has mediation skills. If one partner refuses to go, the other should go alone.

Grandparents can step in with offers of child care and financial assistance if it is needed and appropriate. Our stance needs to be as close to nonjudgmental as we can possibly make it. There are many factors at work in a troubled marriage, and solutions are complicated.

The underlying strategy at this point must be to not take sides. Although we are ready to cast our son-in-law as an ogre, he is still our daughter's husband and will always remain the father of her children. Besides, it gets difficult planning around the needs of an ogre.

Grandchildren may want to paint one or the other parent as a one-dimensional monster, too. But that's the stuff of fairy tales, not real life. We can help them understand that parents make mistakes and parents have to solve them. We can help most by not taking sides. Our grandchildren need to know that although their parents are really steamed at each other right now, they still love their children. We can set a priceless example of civility by letting our grandchildren know that they do not have to stop loving one parent in order to be close to the other.

When our grandchildren voice their deepest fear—What if they decide to divorce?—it's time for another strategy. We must be as optimistic as we possibly can. Remember it's not over till it's over. Whether our adult children decide to separate, divorce, or reconcile, we need to help our grandchildren treat their family with gentleness and compassion.

This optimism is not easy, particularly as the dissolution process proceeds. In a general sense, fighting escalates, and if no solution is found, a period of coldness and noncommunication follows. Words, touch, and glances cease between spouses. Each begins to carve out a separate life and space. This period can last for a short time or a lifetime.

Our grandchildren really begin to show the strain during this period. They can no longer see themselves as a part of their family of origin, and they don't know what the future is going to hold for them. Their behavior deteriorates rapidly. Rudeness, sullenness, school failure, and a generalized lack of energy and interest are common. Our grandchildren are really hurting right now. Their parents are stretched to the max seeing to their own needs. Grandparents can play a valiant role in giving their grandchildren a sense of security, wellness, and self-worth. Grandchildren need to feel that while their family constellation may change, there are many anchors to hold on to during this period.

It may be impossible for grandchildren to put on a social face right now. Continue to ask them to share activities with you, but don't insist. Activities they once loved may lose all appeal. Don't give up! Keep on offering even when the turn-downs are consistent. It takes real self-control to accept no as an answer without trying to persuade or plead. But it is well to remember that sad people are not likely to be very outgoing. Sometimes a telephone call to just say hello, a brief note to let them know we are still thinking of them, or a quick hamburger together can keep our relationship strong during times of stress. If an offer is accepted, rejoice, but don't kill the fatted calf. The

---

TIP: Touch is the universal language of love. When words fail, a hug speaks volumes. If you can't be on the scene, send a teddy bear or other warm fuzzy to your grandchild and tell her it comes with a long-distance hug.

*T*IP: Help your grandchild find something that can be fixed—a running toilet, a broken gate, a peeling front door. Then fix it together.

---

best outings for stressed-out families rely on relaxation, laughter, and casual eating. Fancy dinners, crowds, and mingling with strangers are apt to suffocate. Sometimes our best, most imaginative attempts at cheering up our grandchildren are rebuffed. We can't afford to get hurt feelings. It just makes for more martyrs in a cast of thousands.

As the final decision to divorce is reached, most families are exhausted. There is little feeling of elation or hope. The court process heavily involves the parents, but the grandchildren are often left out of the loop. You can help by explaining how the system works, researching appropriate support groups for children of divorce, and looking for good children's literature that focuses on the problems your grandchildren are experiencing now.

When a child is emotionally vulnerable, as your grandchild is now, a good rule of thumb is to cut his chronological age in half and support him emotionally as if he were that age. Your eight-year-old grandson may want to sit on your lap more, he may need to be heard more quickly, he may hang much closer to his mother or grandmother than before. What he needs most is a heavy dose of "You are a great kid!" and little criticism. If life ever called for a grandparent with open arms and a big smile, this is the time.

This grandchild has been through a lot. And it's not over yet. Now the issues of economics, place of residence, career, and visitation rear their gorgon heads. In the place of so much flux, a loving grandparent can stand out as a rock of constancy and consistency. Continue to offer support, but don't try to take the reins. Ask your child and your grandchild, "How can I help?" And when they tell you, do it.

℘ "My mother was a single parent and had to work all the time to support us. One day I got caught smoking in the girls' bathroom at school. My grandfather was called to come and get me. I was really scared because we didn't get along too good. He assured the principal that it would never happen again. Outside he said to me, 'Everybody makes a mistake once in a while. You have had yours. Do it again, and I'll see that you are grounded for the rest of the school year.' That's all he said. Then he took me out for pizza and I talked to him more than I ever had before. I don't think he ever told my mom. I know I never did. And I never smoked again either."

—Laurie, age 55

Blended Families

When we first greeted our child's new baby, he or she may have been wrapped in a cuddly blanket in the hospital. But when our child becomes a single parent and remarries, we may suddenly be greeting a brand-new grandchild who towers over us, sporting a mohawk haircut and a rose tattoo.

The parents of this new family group think their blending families is a marvelous idea. The children and the grandparents may not equally share their enthusiasm. As grandparents we have the luxury of waiting in the wings to see how it all works out. But our grandchildren are center stage and may not want to speak their lines. One of our grandchildren's greatest irritations may involve sharing—a tough concept that takes a lifetime to learn. They are suddenly being asked to share their parent, their living space, maybe their name, and their future with some adult and kids that they didn't choose.

   🖎 "I was an only child when my mother remarried. My stepbrothers and stepsister were much older than I and busy with their own lives. I was jealous of my stepfather and angry at my mother. It was a miserable period in my life. I think that my grandmother, actually stepgrandmother, helped me more than anyone. She asked me at the reception if I would go shopping with her some day. I said yes, but I meant, 'Over my dead body.' She asked me several more times, and I made excuses. Then one day I came home from school, and there was a letter for me from her. It had an ad for a sale on jeans and one from a pizza place. The note said, 'Be by for you at 4, Love Gramma.' She won, and I went and I have treasured her ever since."

—Marie, age 31

Don't rush in to save the day. If you now enjoy a close relationship with your grandchild, be careful not to dilute it with others. Spend some time alone with your grandchild. She has just experienced a personal invasion that ranks right up there on a scale with Normandy. Listen to her and let her blow off steam, but be a nonjudgmental listener. Help her to evaluate the situation and figure out how changing her own behavior can make life better.

Take care of your grandchild's security needs first, and then begin to build a relationship with your newest grandchild. When your genetic grandchild is feeling comfortable that you are still her nana or gramp, she won't mind helping you get to know the new kid in the house. It's a good idea to ask your genetic grand to clue you in on her new sib and decide what he should call you. Let her tell you what's fun about "Charlie," what's his favorite food, favorite toy, favorite activity. After a bit, ask her to invite Charlie to come along on an outing as her guest. Gradually you can show more affection and interest in the blended family as a whole and in each of its individual members. Guard against forced or rushed intimacy. Children can instantly recognize pretense.

✍ "When Rob married Meg, they had three children between them and another on the way. It didn't do us any good to wring our hands and be upset. We had to see it as our family growing and changing. We had to see these new members as a gift."

—Rita, age 58

Nontraditional Families

Once upon a time almost everybody had a mom and a dad who looked pretty much alike and thought pretty much alike. Dad went out into the world every day and brought back the necessary money to feed and clothe his family. Mom stayed home with the children and helped them with their lessons and baked great cakes. This is a modern-day fairy tale, since things were never that clear-cut and simple. And it's very unlikely that our grandchildren will live like that. Because of unmet social, economic, and psychological needs, many American families are experimenting with living patterns that were unheard of a generation or two ago.

While same-sex marriages are not yet legal, relationships between same-sex partners that endure over time and include children are becoming far more common. Your grandchild may already know somebody who has two dads or two moms.

Single parenthood as a life choice is another social trend. Your grandchild's father or mother may be long gone, a donor, or part of a love affair gone sour. Your grandchild may only know one parent and one set of grandparents.

Your grandchild may be living with a succession of parental partners who come and go without commitment. These partners may attempt to play a parental role with your grandchild.

Your grandchild may grow up in a communal living arrangement that could have a strong religious orientation. In such situations, roles and expectations for each family member may be rigidly assigned. The value system of the group is best preserved by isolating its members from outside influences. It may be very difficult to reach children in these communes.

In each of these situations, children are living family experiences that grandparents probably would not choose for them. In fact, the grandparents may heartily despise the situation. It is of the greatest importance to your grandchildren that you do not let their family situation interfere with your own special relationship. If your son or daughter has chosen one of these situations, you will not influence a change in their behavior through nagging, blaming, or fighting.

In the meantime, grandchildren still need to love and respect their parents, and grandparents should do nothing to weaken the parent-child bond.

> ☙ "I was raised by two women, my mother and her very dear friend whom I called Aunt Peg. We were a family in a community that didn't have much experience with families like ours. As I grew into adolescence, I had to handle some uncomfortable comments and questions about my family. My grandparents are very conservative and traditional people. They never wavered in their support for our family, although it certainly was different from their own. One of my grandmother's favorite sayings is, 'Life is too short to waste a minute being mean.' And she lived it."
>
> —Cheryl, age 20

TIP: Be sensitive when selecting books, dolls, or other toys for your grandchild. There is great variety and ethnic flavor available in today's toy stores.

Three Generations
Under One Roof

In bygone days, several generations of extended family living in one home was a very common arrangement. It worked to cement family bonds while providing a secure lifestyle for maiden aunts, widowed daughters-in-law, and aging or ill grandparents and great-grandparents.

Today, there is a resurgence of three-generation homes. These families are responding to cultural traditions, economic necessities, basic desires, and simple practicality. Among some groups, intergenerational living is the norm rather than the exception.

✍ "When we came from El Salvador, we lived with my husband's cousin and his family. Our first baby was born while we were there. After a while, we got our own apartment, and my husband's parents came to live with us. We are together now for four years. My father-in-law works when he can get outside; my mother-in-law takes care of the house and the children. I have a job and also do the laundry. My husband works and goes to school at night. It is a way that is very good for us. We have love in our home."

—Adelina, age 31

Living together can work very well, but like all life's important commitments, it takes lots of love and lots of effort. A clear understanding of roles and responsibilities together with a large dose of respect can make several generations together a functional and happy family unit.

Grandparents as Parents

Because grandparents care so much about their grand-children, it is logical that the family turns to them when parents cannot parent. Sometimes the parents may be out of the picture entirely, whether temporarily or perma-nently; through death, psychological or physical dysfunc-tion, incarceration, or abandonment. In any of these cases, children and grandparents have lost someone who matters very much to them. That loss and its grief color the relationship that evolves.

Parenting is hard work. It is even harder the second time around. The physical strains are pretty obvious. More laundry, more cooking, less sleep, more responsibilities, less leisure, less freedom, more noise, more litter, less

---

TIP: Take care of yourself. As much as you love your extended family, you and your spouse need time alone. Schedule evening walks by yourselves, take an occasional trip alone, or have dinner out.

money. It sounds like a rotten deal, and it is certainly not a situation that we sought. We were all ready to kick back and enjoy the freedoms of our senior years. Our friends are retiring, traveling, and spending a lot of their time and money on themselves. The only reason a grandparent would take on this responsibility is that love and the need to protect outweigh all the problems so clearly associated with the decision.

✍ "My grandmother, Bubbe, meant everything to me. My dad died when I was real little, and my mom had to work. Parents are always worried about something. They haven't really grown up yet themselves. But grandparents, they just love you and accept you. She was always there for me. There was nothing—nothing—that I needed that she didn't give me. When I was sick, she would sit right by my bed with me all night if I needed her. She is dying now, and my mom and I take turns sitting by her bed."

—Emile, age 19

TIP: Try writing a contract with your adolescent or older grandchildren that covers the essentials on exactly how you will live together. It's a good way to jointly problem solve and set parameters that everyone can live with.

Grandparents need to know right up front that this experience will be very different from their first parenting experience. The first big difference is that these children know they had a real parent. Children always deal better with the truth. A lie may seem kinder, but it requires constant maintenance and it really doesn't help anyone in the long run. Instead, help your grandchildren to know all the good things about their parents. Share their parents' frailties but with a heavy dose of compassion. Children can accept that their parents have faults, but they cannot accept the fact that their parents are no good. Encourage your grandchildren to see their parents or write to them or phone them if possible. If the parent is simply missing, help your grandchild keep a journal of his life and feelings to share with that parent one day.

☞ "Three years ago, I was about to retire and move to Alabama to be with my sister. But my daughter was having a tough time with drugs and her husband leaving and all. She couldn't afford to keep those kids, and she wasn't in any shape to do it either. Then she OD'd and ended up in the hospital. I ended up with my grandkids. Someone had to take them, and I was the likely choice. I wasn't real happy about it at first. I mean, I was so close to leaving and all. But I spent a lot of time talking to the Lord, and He convinced me it was all in His plan.

"So now I've got four kids again. They give me a tough time sometimes, but they listen to me. It's hard keeping up with them. I'm learnin' about Snoop Doggy Dog and rappers and baggy clothes. It's different this time. One thing's for sure, none of those kids are going to get messed up on drugs. I won't let them. I make them all write to their Momma, and I took the oldest two to see her in rehab. Alabama will be there, but these kids couldn't wait."

—Emma, age 63

As if the emotional needs were not enough, there are the sheer practicalities to deal with. Grandparents who parent just can't be as heroic as they might be if they were grandparents with separate homes and lives. When we parent grandchildren, we're the ones who have to get them to finish their homework and brush their teeth; we have to remind them of consequences and limits. We are going to see more negativism and resistance in our grandchildren. It's not us personally. Children just have to do a certain amount of fighting with adults who try to control them.

Grandchildren have even more ammunition to hurl at grandparents who parent. We may be too old to be their parent, and they will tell us so again and again. We went to school a century ago and don't have a clue about today's schoolroom. Our values are ancient, carved on the Rosetta stone, and nobody thinks like that anymore. And the final blow: "My father [or my mother] would let me/would help me/wouldn't treat me like this." The power and greatness of an absent parent can grow in our grandchildren's imagination. This parent assumes a Prince Charming mystique. "Someday my dad will come and whisk me away from all this."

Here are some tips from grandparents who are valiantly struggling to parent their grandchildren:

1. Don't make life harder than it has to be. Buy ready-made Halloween costumes or packaged cookies or carryout food. Get all the help that's available from others and save your energy for helping your grandchild feel secure and loved.

2. Don't compare this to your first parenting experience. You are different, the situation is different, and so is the child.

3. Get to know the people who matter in your grandchild's life: friends and their parents, coaches, teachers, Scout leaders, and so on. The more you know of her world, the wider your network of assistance and the better you understand her needs and wants.

4. Keep your own circle of friends and your own pleasures. Don't deny yourself the fun that you might otherwise be enjoying.

5. Take care of your own physical and mental health. If you need a break, arrange it. Both

you and your grandchild may deserve it. No one benefits if you wear yourself out.

6. Get to know others who share your experience. Grandparents-as-parents groups exist across the country. If there is no such organization in your area, start one. Arrange discussion groups, toy swaps, picnics, baby-sitting co-ops. Talk and laugh and complain to each other.

7. Do what you do out of love. Don't expect gratitude. Children have no control over the circumstances of their lives. Fate has cast them and you into these roles. Never make them feel guilty about events over which they had no control.

8. Feel very good about yourself. In doing your very best for your grandchildren, you are helping to endow them with a sense of personal worth that will see them through the road ahead.

No matter how different your children's family is from the family in which you grew and flourished, the basic human needs for love and approval are always the same. Grandparents who knew the power of the special bond between grandparent and grandchild can pass those same feelings of magic to this grandchild. Your relationship with your grandchild provides the underlying fabric for whatever design is assembled in your quilt of family. You are the thread that holds it all together.

6

God Bless You, Tiny Tim

❖

Grandparenting
for Special Needs

*T*iny Tim was the very heart of the Cratchit family. His courage, cheerfulness, and compassion under difficult circumstances brought out the very best in his family and even touched the stony heart of Scrooge. We all hope for perfection in our children, but physical or mental imperfection does not rob a person of value, lovability, or personal achievement. Grandparenting the Tiny Tims of the world is a calling for those of great heart and wisdom, those who see past the exterior to the potential in each child.

✍ "I was so upset when they told me that my granddaughter was born blind. At first, all I could think of was what she couldn't do. It took me a while to realize that she had a wonderful sense of humor, more determination than most of us, and a way about her that is just charming. That child has truly been the light of my life."

—Myrna, age 61

Childhood Illness

When a newborn is too small or ill to leave the hospital, the whole family feels cheated. The new parents are over-whelmed with disappointment, guilt, and sheer exhaus-tion from hospital procedures and protocols. Grandparents can be the rock the whole family needs as their world drifts from its moorings.

Even though you may be combating your own fears and frustrations, offer the love and encouragement your adult children need. Educate yourself past fear to action, and offer your assistance where it is needed.

Siblings, too, are disappointed but also disgruntled. They naturally resent the new stranger for the upheaval in their world and for stealing parental attention. They are not displaying inhuman indifference; they are reacting as children. You can blunt their anger and frustration by devising activities that help the family as a whole. Grand-parents can help their grandchildren take care of the house for Mom, make a meal for the family, or write cheer-them-up cards for their parents. When the new baby is ready to

TIP: Give a gift to your older grandchildren from their hospitalized sibling. Put on the card, "To the best brother [or sister] in the world."

---

come home, you can help your grandchildren plan a homecoming celebration.

Accidents and critical or chronic illness can strike children at any time. We all hope the odds will never find our loved ones, but sometimes they do. This kind of stress is also critical to a family unit. Many a family flounders and fails under the attendant burden of guilt, anxiety, and expense. Grandparents can become the glue that helps to hold a family together while they battle the faceless enemy.

Your grown children may feel that they have failed their most fundamental responsibility as parents: protecting and guarding their children. They hurt and suffer with their sick child, bear the burden of what-ifs, try to comfort the frightened siblings at home, and worry about mounting bills. Grandparents have many vital roles to play here. First wipe out the what-ifs; they no longer matter. What matters is facing the situation and dealing with it. Give your grown children a heavy dose of optimism and support. They can make it through because they must, and you will help them.

They don't want to admit it but they need a break. You can offer to sit with your sick grandchild while his parents shower, sleep, or take a walk. You can bake their favorite cookies and include them in a care package with some cologne, a funny book, a set of tapes, a new sweater. Offer to take the siblings for pizza and a movie and give their parents some quiet time at home. If you cannot be there physically, consider picking up part of the cost of a housekeeper or a mother's helper to lighten the load and keep things normal in your grandchild's household.

Your healthy grandchildren are also hurting at this time. When a sibling falls seriously ill, healthy brothers and sisters are stunned by guilt. Children reach back into history and dredge up all the awful things they ever said, did, or even thought about their sick sib. And then they assume responsibility for the illness—as though their actions or thoughts somehow caused it.

Caring, sensitive grandparents can focus time, energy, and attention on the healthy grandchildren and help to keep them that way. Their day-to-day needs are not suspended. They still need haircuts and new shoes, to attend birthday parties, soccer practice, field trips—all the things that make for normal living. They need attention

---

TIP: Go to a library or bookstore and get the best books you can find for children and adults dealing with your particular family circumstance. Ignorance is far more frightening than knowledge. Children, particularly, need to have their imagination countered with information.

and the strokes that make them feel the family still cares about them.

✍ "My younger brother had leukemia when he was little. I remember feeling that somehow I made him sick. It was awful. I felt that I shouldn't ever do anything fun again. One day, when we all came home from the clinic, there were two brand-new bikes on the front porch. I bolted from the car. I had wanted a bike so badly, but I thought it was wrong to ask for one. There was a card on my bike for both of us. It said, 'I love you both, Grandma Betsy.' I remember turning to my mother and saying, 'This is the happiest day of my life.' "

—James, age 22

Your sick grandchild needs you to be unchanged for her. She needs to feel that she is a normal kid with an illness. Continue your relationship as normally as you are able—loving notes and calls, visits to the hospital where you share well-loved books again, playful humor that lets this grandchild know that you have not despaired. Sustain your grandchild with quiet companionship and shared familiar activities.

✍ "I was a very sickly kid. I was in and out of hospitals most of my life. My folks were really worried about me. I felt like they were hovering over me all of the time, worrying about my medicine. My grandfather was the one who made me feel normal. He would call just to tell me a joke or a riddle. A couple of times a week, he would send me a cartoon in the mail. He never talked about my health problems but would always say something like, 'How's it shaking, buddy?' "

—George, age 19

Developmental Disabilities

Equally great adjustments are needed when a child is diagnosed as developmentally disabled. There are good times and bad, emotional highs and lows. Parents can feel anger, denial, sadness, fear, guilt, or shame. They may also feel great relief that a name has finally been given to the unvoiced fears they have had over the years. Suddenly a child called lazy has real learning disabilities. A child called willful has a hearing deficit.

Parents can find it difficult to be objective about their own children. Grandparents, one step removed from this grandchild, can see a little more clearly. This clarity, combined with love, can sustain a family as it struggles to accommodate the special needs of one of its children.

Practice empathy, not sympathy. Diagnosis of a

*T*IP: Become active in your local Special Olympics. Encourage any and all of your grandchildren to participate with you.

---

disability does not cast that child as a tragic figure and a huge burden for the family. In reality, these kids have some special needs and do require some special accommodations, but they have far more similarities than differences with every other child. Grandparents need to see them first as children, then move on to perceiving their strengths and weaknesses.

Again, knowledge is the best antidote to fear. The more you learn about the problem, the clearer your perspective. Subscribe to *Exceptional Parent,* and send a subscription to your adult children. Look for lectures and support groups in your area and continually seek new information. Grandparents can assist with various therapies and educational programs. These activities can become drudgery for child and parent. A little dose of grandparenting magic can transform them into something special.

There are specialists galore ready to focus on your grandchild's problems. Grandparents need to focus on the normal things he does. Notice and support his sense of humor, assertiveness, individuality, or creativity. This grandchild may also be just as naughty and manipulative as any of your other grandchildren, and you need to react impartially. Be sure to mention to his parents that you see this as quite normal.

❧ "When Johnny wraps his arms around my neck and gives me one of his world-class smiles, my heart about bursts with pleasure. He may never learn to read, but he has taught this whole family, from Grandpa on down, the real meaning of life and of love. I can't imagine life without him."
—Al, age 64

Progress can be very slow for this grandchild. Grandparents noticing positive changes should celebrate the progress they see. Both your grandchild and his parents will appreciate hearing that you see improvement. A grandparent's encouragement can push a child to fight even harder to overcome his problems.

Above all else, love this special grandchild just as you do any others you may have. Strive to show no favoritism or rejection. This grandchild wants to be loved.

TIP: A note to your adult children saying, "It was wonderful to see Tommy doing so much better at . . ." can brighten the day of a family with a special child.

✍ "My younger brother had Down's syndrome, and he needed a lot of care. When I was about 11, I went through a time when I didn't want my new friends to know about him. I loved him, but I was ashamed of him. My parents noticed and tried to talk to me. I wound up feeling guilty on top of ashamed.

"It was my grandfather who helped me most of all. He took me for a walk and said, 'There are very few really special people on this earth and your brother is one of them. He is completely honest and pure in how he feels and how he acts. You are another of the really special people. You have been chosen to help all of the others learn to understand him and to love him.' I never felt so close to someone as I did at that moment with my grandfather."

—Ellen, age 29

For these children, the teenage years can often be tougher than any others. As they are struggling to find their emerging selves, the constraints of society can be very difficult to live with. Coming of age means coming to terms with one's self, future prospects, and potential pitfalls. Small wonder that teens are scared to look in the mirror. Their self-doubt can result in an overwhelming sense of unhappiness. Experimentation with smoking, alcohol, and drugs to find relief and the companionship of others is not uncommon.

❧ "When I was a teenager, I tried to kill myself. I wasn't happy. I got angry and embarrassed when it didn't work. I didn't want to see anybody. But Grandfather came anyway. I told him I didn't know what to say. He said, 'Let's just hold each other for a while.' He never asked me why I tried to kill myself. I'm real glad I'm still alive today."

—Celine, age 23

Grandparents' Health Problems

Just as grandchildren can have special needs, so too can grandparents. Our own hopes for invincibility prevent us from thinking about personal illness until it happens. Sooner or later, we know illness may show, and when it does, grandparents need to remember that children deal best with the truth. That truth should be tailored to the ages of our grandchildren and their need to know.

You should use simple and direct language in describing a medical condition to your grandchildren. You should be optimistic but unafraid to show your feelings. Their fears are validated when they know you're scared, too.

❧ "When my grandmother got sick, she took me aside to tell me what was wrong with her. She got kind of teary, but she told me everything straight out about her cancer. She said she was scared, but with our help she'd make it through. She was a really strong lady who taught all of us how to look life square in the eyes."

—Helen, age 31

Whether you are grandparenting from a walker, wheelchair, bed, or hospital room, you can give to your grandchildren what they want most: attention, true and undivided. As long as you can look into your grandchildren's eyes and listen to their words, you can reinforce their sense of self-worth and encourage their development.

"Nana was bedridden when I was a little kid. She lived with us. Every night she would invite me to come and watch TV with her. I would sit on the corner of her pillow and drink grape soda and eat pretzels. I was in charge of the remote control. We always had a good time together. I never thought of it back then, but I bet I left a lot of crumbs in her bed. She never said anything."

—Christian, age 16

TIP: Demystify medical equipment for your grandchildren. Allow them to try out your walker or take a spin in your wheelchair.

From our grandchildren's perspective, the disabled or infirm grandparent may be the most essential of all because he is available all of the time. He's not out working, shopping, or playing golf. He can focus solely on their companionship. Our grandchildren will also accomplish a sense of competency in that they are helping instead of always being helped. Often this type of relationship is the most cherished of all.

✍ "My mother was wonderful. She was paralyzed from the neck down and required total care— feeding, dressing, blowing her nose. When she contracted cancer, her condition deteriorated rapidly. Yet, she was always happy to listen to a story, watch a cartoon, share a bite of peanut butter sandwich with her grandchildren. She made no demands of them but truly basked in their presence. They helped her, and she told me how happy they made her feel.

"When she died, they mourned her deeply. They remembered only the positive things about her. One would have to ask a lot of questions before the facts of her disability came out. Not because they were hiding the truth, but because the disability was not important to them. In addition to showing love, affection, attention, and joy to her grandchildren, she taught them lessons for life as no one else could. She taught them to live with dignity, to face adversity with courage, to lose with grace, to focus on what one can do instead of on what one can't do, and to find peace despite enormous obstacles. Her grandchildren are more caring, genuine people because of her. What a shame it would have been to have lost all of this because she was severely disabled."

—Emily, age 57

Children can understand emotional or cognitive disability as well. They will help if they are told how to do so. Take the time to explain what has happened and what they can expect. When grandchildren are included in this manner, they are called upon to be their very best, and they rise to the occasion. They learn to accept people for what they are and not to compare and complain. They learn not to fear the realities of life and that they can successfully handle tough situations. Most importantly, they learn that love extends far beyond what we can give or do and into what we are. This experience helps children grow into adults with confidence and a generosity of spirit.

Preparation for visiting grandparents in nursing homes or hospitals paves the way for a comfortable visit. One way to reduce the strangeness of a new environment is to share tiny artifacts of that environment in advance. Bring home the paper cups pills are dispensed in, unused jelly portions from hospital or nursing home trays, and so on. Draw a map of how to find Grandma or Grandpa's room from the hospital entrance and let your grandchildren follow it. Ask them to help by refilling flower vases, arranging all the plants and flowers in the window, adjusting window shades, or filling a water cup. Ask your grandchildren to talk about their friends, sports, and school. Keep the visit short and sweet.

A Death in the Family

Death enters every family. It could be tomorrow, or it could be years from now. It could be a friend, a sibling, a parent, a grandparent, or a pet. Whatever the circumstances, death is a fact of life, and it should not and cannot be hidden from your grandchildren.

As a nation, Americans have a great deal of difficulty confronting death. We tend to say someone has "passed away" or "rests in peace." Even though it's difficult, it's best to be honest. Although the truth should be tailored to the age and development of each of your grandchildren, telling them the pure and simple truth about death is the best strategy. They should be included in family plans as much as possible.

Children take great comfort from the ceremonies and traditions that grow out of our culture and heritage. Allow your grandchildren to accompany the family to religious or secular services. Although younger children do not need to view embalmed bodies, older children should be permitted to do so when they have been made to understand what to expect.

❧ "My grandparents shared a true love story. They were engaged on Valentine's Day. Their special song was 'My Funny Valentine.' Everyone in our family knew that song because they sang it so often. Grandma had a series of heart attacks and small strokes that left her bedridden. Gramp would ask my sisters and me to sing their song to her . . . so many times as she slowly died. When it happened, we were as prepared as a family can be to lose someone so special. Gramp asked Sharon and me to sing 'My Funny Valentine' at the funeral. It was really hard, but we did it."

—Allison, age 33

Adults who stifle the natural urge to mourn hurt themselves. Adults who stifle a child's natural urge to mourn hurt them as well. Grief has a pattern of sadness, listlessness, sleeplessness, and loss of appetite. Grief has no set timetable.

Recovery from the death of a loved one is a gradual process for everyone. Being able to talk about your grief

---

TIP: Help your grandchild select, plant, and tend a shrub as a living memorial. Make a plaque together to mark the shrub.

helps to heal it. Further healing comes from taking real steps to deal with that grief.

With this in mind, you can help your grandchildren to make scrapbooks or flower arrangements in memory of the person who has died. You can help them write journal entries, letters, poems, and stories that illustrate their feelings. Grandchildren can shop, bake, cook, and deliver food to help others who mourn. When death comes to your family, hold your grandchild's hand and her heart as you mourn your losses together.

✍ "I grew up in my grandparents' home. My Grandma Cooper used to read the Bible in the morning and evening every day of her life. She taught me how to make preserves, and we spent a lot of time together. She taught me how to shop. She had a way of making me feel special. She was always saying things like, 'You reap what you sow' and 'Treat others as you want to be treated.' She died on Thanksgiving eve.

"I brought her furniture home with me after she died, and it's a consistent reminder of what she meant to me. I have a lamp on my table that belonged to her. She got it for green stamps and I helped her put those stamps in the book. Every Thanksgiving I think of her and what she meant to me."

—Paige, age 47

Just as Tiny Tim was an inspiration to his family and those around him, we can be the inspiration that our grandchildren need to see beyond the troubles of life to the joy and growth that can come from surmounting those troubles. Life is not fair, nor does it play favorites. Each of us will deal with troubles on a major scale sometime in our life. Grandparents can show their grandchildren the way to acquire grace under fire and how to develop the strength that is needed to keep our families whole and healthy no matter what adversity we face.

7

Electric Granny Stays Plugged In

❖

Grandparenting over Long Distances

Skipping through the woods to Grandmother's house is out of the question for most grandchildren. We don't live in friendly villages anymore. Our world has expanded enormously over the last few generations. Some of us now work for multinational corporations. We go where our job takes us or where the jobs are. Thankfully, grandparenting is highly portable.

Even if we're lucky enough to reach out and physically touch our grandchildren today, odds are we'll probably be reaching out with Ma Bell before their childhood is over. Very few of us will spend our lives working at the same job or living in the same town where we grew up. Most of us will retire somewhere where the living is easier and more economical. Either they will move or we will. Learning to be an electric granny or grampy is essential if we are to maintain our grandparenting bonds.

It takes more imagination and effort to grandparent long distance, but the potential for magic is still there. Limiting our grandparenting to holiday visits or birthday mailings is a mistake. Continual correspondence, calls, and little gifts are what plug us into our distant grandchildren's lives.

᠕❤ "Nana knew how much I loved to get mail when I was a little kid. She used to buy me things from catalogs and use my name. That got my name on all these mailing lists. I got more mail sometimes than my parents. She was really an awesome lady."
—Justin, age 16

No child living ever gets enough mail. Adults may get irritated by junk mail, but kids would die to be on Ed McMahon's mailing list—all those wonderful stamps! Traveling grandparents can drop a postcard in the mail from airports around the country and around the world. Your grandchild will think the mail carrier is your personal messenger and will never tire of the cards that you send. Box up and send an album to preserve your first correspondence. Your grandchild will look at her postcards again and again when she is little. As she grows older, that album continues to say, "My grandparents thought I was neat."

TIP: Send a picture book about children and grand-parents. Include a picture of yourself glued inside the book. As your grandchild looks at pictures of grand-parents, he will see a picture of his very own grand-parents.

"My grandparents didn't live around us. But when I was growing up, every week, sometimes twice a week, I'd get an envelope in the mail. It always had some crazy, funny return address on it: some-times Captain Marvel, sometimes the president, sometimes just a goofy name. It was always writ-ten in green ink. Inside, I'd find a cartoon, a dollar bill, a few sticks of gum, a sticker . . . all kinds of wonderful stuff. My daughter just had her first baby. I've already stocked up on green pens."

—Lucy, age 45

No doubt about it, return mail is gratifying. But it shouldn't be the motivation for writing to your grands. Adults can dash off a note without thinking twice about it. Kids may not be comfortable with writing letters until they are in high school or beyond. Understanding this fact before you begin a correspondence with your grandchild will diminish the chances of hurt feelings and resentment when your mailbox isn't loaded with return correspon-dence.

You can take steps to increase the odds of developing a mutual correspondence by sending a hefty bunch of stamped, self-addressed mailers to your grandchild. When they are very little, ask them to send you a drawing for your refrigerator. Nothing is as wonderful for the child and easy on the parents as a stack of mailers all addressed and ready to go into the mailbox. As they get older, you can ask for one of their school papers, one of their favorite Sunday comics, or the schedule of their sports league. None of these things require extra writing. Actually, they are more informative than a laboriously composed letter that says: "Dear Grama, Wish yu wer hear. We miss yu. We are fin. Your grandkid."

If you are awaiting the birth of a grandchild, purchase a cassette tape player as one of your presents to the expectant couple. Record some Mother Goose rhymes or your favorite story or song. Grandma or Grandpa's voice could be the one that puts him to sleep at night. Your infant grandchild will know your voice before he even sees your face. As he grows, include a copy of the book you've recorded. Start a taped correspondence with your grand-

---

TIP: Send a box of dress-ups to your grandchild— old hats, fur pieces, jewelry, or pieces of fancy material. Include a disposable camera and ask for photos of your grand in her fancy outfits for your refrigerator.

child when he starts preschool. Record a story for him
and include a personal message asking him to record
something—a message, song, or story—and send it back
to you. Don't expect a thirty-minute tape but be happy
with the breathy ninety-second conversation you get.
Include a mailer, so he can go to the mailbox and send it
himself. Record your answer, and you've begun a long-
distance conversation that can continue throughout his
childhood.

✍ "My dad was always a great storyteller. When we
visited with him the last time, we got him to
record some of the stories he was telling the kids.
They listened to those stories all the way home
in the car. They ask for them sometimes at bed-
time, too."

—Sarah, age 33

The key to distant grandparents' success is inventively
reminding your grandchildren that you think about them
every day, that they are always a part of your thoughts.
Enforce this concept by sending your older grandchild a
disposable camera and asking for photos that show "A day
in the life of. . . ." Have him take photos of his everyday
experiences: waiting with his chums for the school bus,
lunch mayhem, soccer practice, walking the dog, saying
good night to Mom and Dad. You can send him return
photos of your own day—Grampa going to work, the

*T*IP: Write your grandchild a story about something that you do every day. Draw a picture of Grandpa in the morning and label it "Grandpa woke up." Draw pictures and simple explanations of your daily routine. Staple the pages together and send them to your grandchild.

---

office gang, your house and neighborhood, pets—so that he is familiar with your lives.

✍ "My grandfather has collected stamps since he was a boy. When I was little, he used to show me his stamp albums. When I got older, he helped me start a collection of my own. He would take me to the shop and sell a stamp once in a while and that really made me interested. Stamps have helped us get to know one another really well, even though we don't live very close together."
—Randy, age 15

Modern technology is definitely on the side of the long-distance grandparent. Photocopiers, computers, fax machines, answering machines—all these gizmos can be used for the grandparenting cause.

You can share your heritage with your grandchild across the miles. Photocopy old family photos. The irreplaceable originals are intact, but you can send your

*T*IP: Draw a family tree and decorate the branches with photocopies of the photos of your grandchild's forebears. Try to include both sides of the tree. Photocopy the original piece and send one to each grandchild as they arrive.

---

grandchild pictures of old Uncle Horace standing by his Model T to tack on his wall. Include Horace's history on the back of the picture. Add the good stuff and the goofy stuff about Horace. You want your family tree to sparkle, not loom. Make your grandchild the keeper of the family archives. Everyone wants to know what genetic stock is cooking in their veins. It would be fun to send copies of heirloom pictures and photos of both your own and your child's growing years.

Camcorders offer a wonderful way to exchange and enjoy experiences. In addition to filming real trips and happenings, you can record yourself doing mock TV commercials, retelling weird experiences, or just talking to your grandkids. You can ask them to do the same and exchange tapes to play at home.

‹♥ "When I was recovering from surgery, I received a video tape from my 16-year-old grandson in the mail. He and his friends had decided that since I wasn't getting out, they'd share one of their nights out with me. They recorded their trip to the local

hangout, gave me a tour—including the men's john—and introduced me to all of their friends. The ones I had previously met all wished me a speedy recovery. Then they took me line dancing at a local dance hall and I laughed as they recorded themselves being kicked out for being underage. Then they drove me home. By the time they said good night to me at the front door, I had tears in my eyes. It was one of the best nights out I ever had. I must have played that tape a hundred times."

—Martha, age 68

If you know that your grandchild will be home at a certain time each day, call during that period at least once a week. Chat about your days. If she is home alone after school, this is a perfect time to call. Knowing you will call at a certain time gives her a sense of security. Let her initiate a collect call every so often. If she's not at home, leave a message just for her on the answering machine. If

---

𝒯IP: Send a disposable camera to younger grands and ask them to take pictures of their favorite people and places. Include a stamped, self-addressed envelope so they can return the camera to you for processing. Return the favor with pictures of your own favorite places, people, and animals.

the phone company offers a cheap deal for dialing your closest friends, make your grandchild one of those friends. Some savvy (and generous) grandparents have even gotten themselves an 800 number so that expense is not an issue on incoming calls from the grands.

Offer to help him with a project at school. Fax him needed information that will round out his report. If you're both computer literate, get on one of the networks together and drop e-mail to each other.

Send little gifts that will keep on giving to your friendship with this child. Share a magazine subscription. If he likes cars, subscribe to the same magazine for both of you. Call and talk about the newest issue. If your grandchild is interested in animals, subscribe to a zoo magazine. Or go to the zoo yourself and take pictures of the animals to send. Promise to go together when he comes to visit. Many zoos have adopt-an-animal programs. Why not adopt one together? Read a good children's book and send a copy to your grandchild. Talk about the book together. Get fan club photos of his favorite sports star and send them on. Ask what music he likes. Buy a coveted tape or CD and listen to it before you send it to him. You can understand your grandchild much better if you understand his interests—and you'll be widening your horizons, too.

🖎 "I like basketball. My grandmother likes basketball, too. She travels a lot. Every time she goes somewhere, she sends me something from wherever she went. When I started playing basketball, she started sending me basketball stuff—team shirts, caps, mugs, pennants, and programs from different cities and colleges. It's fun to have them even though I don't wear all of them. When she finds something really neat, she usually calls to tell me about it so I can be on the lookout for it, but sometimes she surprises me.

"When it's NCAA time, she really goes crazy. She calls me before all the games to compare notes on the players and who's going to win, then she calls me afterward to see what I thought of the game. We have a good time sharing basketball."

—Kevin, age 16

Clue your grandchild in on your life as well. Archaeologists can reconstruct a whole civilization on the basis of a few bits of broken pottery. You can send your grandchild tidbits of your life. When you travel, collect the free soaps and shampoo from the hotel and send them to your grandchild. Little kids love them because they are child-sized. Older girls love them because they smell good and are different from the everyday soaps at home. All the free stuff you pick up in your travels provides an opportunity to share with your grandchild. When the bank gives out pocket calendars, send yours to your grandchild. When you get a silly little umbrella in your exotic drink, send it

*T*IP: To help your grandchild get to know you long distance, try sending her installments of "My Life as a Child." Include the tough subjects you couldn't master, your heroes, the scrapes you got into, your most embarrassing moments, the aunt or uncle who drove you crazy, the beloved relative, your career fantasies, the simple pleasures of growing up.

---

as a treasure to your grandchild. When your fashion magazine oozes with perfume ads, send them to your grandchild to scratch and sniff.

"When my grandfather traveled, he would always send me a souvenir spoon from wherever he was. They were all real tacky and inexpensive. But when I was a little kid, they were the crown jewels. I had this marvelous collection of spoons for teas with my dolls. When friends were over, I'd bring out my spoons for dessert. I had a couple of really special ones, and if I was mad at my friends, I wouldn't bring those out. I had one that I really loved from Japan. I wouldn't let anyone else use that spoon."

—Lorelei, age 22

When you know your grandchild's life is at a low ebb, find some long-distance, nonintrusive ways to cheer him up. Send a goofy card, a funny book, silly Band-Aids, or the old standby, a box of chocolates. Gentle humor is one of the best antidotes for pain. This is the time when you can really become a fairy godmother or godfather. Send him a card that somehow tells him he is a really valuable kid. Sign it "A secret admirer." When your grandchild is older and feeling the blues of adolescence, figure out some way to make him feel better. A bouquet of balloons delivered after school on his birthday or a pizza to share with his gang adds stature to flagging egos.

℘ "When my grandchild was little, she had some tough times, like all kids do. I used to send her cards and little surprises. I would sign them, 'From your secret buddy.' When friends of mine went out of town, I'd give them a card or a little package to send to her. She never figured out who her secret buddy was, but getting those cards was always so exciting for her. She used to try and guess who her buddy was. She still hasn't figured it out."

—Mabel, age 72

All of us are busy these days. Clever entrepreneurs now offer services tailor-made for busy grandparents. We can now mail-order food baskets, flowers, candygrams, or giant cans of pretzels and popcorn. Coming home from school to a basket of fruit or a can of popcorn is almost like sharing cookies and milk with us. Enclose a message with your gift that rings positive. Instead of the hackneyed "Wish I were there," go for "I was just thinking of you," because what you want them to know is that you really do think about them a lot.

    "My grandfather gave me a credit card on my sixteenth birthday. Can you believe it? But, wait, there were ground rules. It wasn't carte blanche, but he would cover twenty dollars a month on that card. 'I'd spend that much on you if we lived close by,' he explained. 'This way we can do things even if we aren't together.' I never took advantage of that privilege, and I never used that card without thinking about that great old guy."

—Jack, age 26

Sharing over the miles the smallest details of your world and little mementos that say you are thinking of them sets the stage for the way you will spend time when you are actually face-to-face with your grandchild. You have been getting to know each other without regard to distance and will not meet as strangers.

    "Since I don't live close to my only grandchild, I feel that I have some homework to do in keeping up with how she might be changing between visits. I watch kids' TV once in a while to try to stay current, read the kids' pages in the paper, and try to learn what other children her age are doing and liking. That way, I am better prepared to get on her level when I see her. It also makes me feel a little closer to her because I think I understand better."

—Nina, age 46

Distances and the cost of covering them mean that getting to Grandma's house is an event in itself for some families. Why not share the cost and meet someplace in the middle?

✍ "One of my best memories of a family get-together was when my mom bought a weekend at a ski resort at a church auction. My sister's family and mine trooped up to the mountains together. Everyone was excited. It was a big place, with plenty of room. When we got there, it was clean, and somebody else cleaned up when we left. It was so much easier. We just spent the time together having fun."

—Cathy, age 52

Break out of the traditional mold and make short visits that don't always center around holidays or big family events. Both grandparents don't have to go for every visit. If your mate is off on a golf trip and you have a free weekend, head off to see the kids. Business travel can sometimes bring you close enough to schedule a quick visit on your way home. If your plane schedule is such that you can plan a layover in the airport close to your grandchildren, arrange to meet for a sandwich in the airport. When your grandchild goes to camp, see if you can't arrange a weekend visit. It could mean the difference between extended homesickness and a good camp experience. Make all the necessary arrangements ahead of time, so the camp knows who you are and you have permission to spend time with your grandchild.

&✿ "My grandparents did all kinds of things for me. I remember one night when they showed up at a fourth-grade play. It was a complete surprise. They had driven five hours to get there. They clapped loud and long at the curtain call and gave me one long-stemmed rose. I felt like a queen. They told me I was wonderful. Of course, I only had a bit part. But they made me feel that I was a star."

—Kim, age 26

Grandparents can give a grandchild a wonderful gift and sneak in some really intense grandparenting by offering to have one grandchild come and stay for a weekend or a week. Plan some really special activity—see a baseball game, go fishing, or go to an amusement park. But spend most of your time in easy activities that let you get even closer to your grandchild.

✍ "When Gramma is coming to visit, she and the kids plan a special day away from us. They scheme by telephone a week or so in advance and have it all planned out, so that is one day my wife and I have free. The kids get really excited about their plans, and my wife and I get really excited about the free time, too."

—John, age 40

All grandparents can learn to listen to their grandchildren in a way that permits hearing not only their words but the meaning behind those words. Children know what they need. Once you know what that is, you can act to really make a difference.

✍ "I love it most of all when my grandparents come to visit during the week. We don't have to go to day care. We get to stay home and just play. I love that the best."

—Alex, age 10

Electric granny is just everyday granny in disguise. We have the same opportunities to get to know our grandchildren whether they are close or far away. We can let them know in a thousand little ways how much they mean to us, now and forever. Through the mail and over the air waves we can pass on to them our sense of humor, our values, and our family history. Distance is not an insurmountable problem. With imagination and effort we can become a major part of their basic circuitry.

Tips for Long-Distance Grandparenting

For Younger Grands

- Send easy-to-understand information about the stars, and call to see which constellations your grandchild can see in her sky and which ones you can see.
- Write a simple story about your grandchild, and send him monthly installments.
- Send a picture of your pet and a little note about something funny or wonderful that your pet does.
- Cut out pictures from glossy magazines or a few funny stickers and mail them with a short note.
- Send a packet of seeds that can be planted in a pot on the windowsill or in their garden. Plant the same seeds and call and compare notes on the growth of your plants.
- Send photographs of your neighborhood and your home. When your grandchild visits, she will feel that she already knows your neighborhood.
- If you feed the birds, send your grandchild a birdfeeder for his yard or a birdhouse. Call and

ask what birds come to the feeder or have made a home in the birdhouse. Send him pictures of the birds you feed in your yard.

- Draw a picture of you and your grandchild doing something together—blowing bubbles, reading, walking, cooking—and promise to do this when she next visits you.

For Elementary School Grands

- Send simple craft kits to make planters, kaleidoscopes, or simple science experiments. If the age listed on the box is older than your grand, choose another item. The age suggested is also a safety guide and should not be ignored.
- With parental OK, send an outdoor plant to be your grandchild's own tree or bush, against which he can gauge his growth.

For Preteens

- Pay for a course in something that interests her—karate, ice-skating, watercolors, sewing, cooking, computers.
- Ask for his advice on which movies to see. Follow that advice and talk about the movie.
- Plan activities for her next visit. Let her choose the activities and stick with the plan.

- Ask for pictures of him and his friends. Send a disposable camera. Don't judge by appearances.
- When you are making charitable contributions, ask for her advice on which groups she thinks are worthy. Make a contribution in her name.
- Send a cookbook of your best recipes. Ask for a care package of your cookie recipe.
- Ask for advice on getting a new hairstyle or buying a new outfit. Ask which colors he thinks would look best on you. Follow his advice.
- Send a tape of your favorite music, your best fishing lure, or pictures of your first car. Send pictures of her parents at her age. Send pictures of yourself at her age.

For Teens

- Tell your grandteen the story behind a family heirloom and give it to him.
- Collect the photographs that you have of your grandchild from birth until now. Put them in an album and share it with her.
- If you are trading in your stereo system or automobile for a newer model and can afford it, ask your grandteen if he would like your hand-me-down.

8

Wise Owl's Foresight Was in Demand

❖

Putting Grandparenting Experience to Work

When disaster loomed on the horizon, Winnie-the-Pooh beat a path to Owl's tree. Owl was a problem solver. Not only did he foresee problems, he helped others work through their own difficulties and find solutions. Through our years of experience and real-life problem solving, we have earned our stripes. This wisdom enables us to not only model the values we grew up with and instill them in the next generation but also to take positive action to prevent accidents and instill caution. Our vigilant role begins with protecting our young grandchildren from potential hazards and ends with helping them learn how to protect themselves.

Having raised our own children, we have the inside line for preparedness when it comes to grandchildren.

We've already done it all! Only one thing has truly changed. We're grandparents now. We have earned the privilege of loving, enjoying, and helping our grandchildren.

Grandchildren in Our Home

Our home is our castle. As our children have grown, we've moved beyond practical decorating. No more mud browns and grass greens! We've become free to decorate in pastels and unpack and display the treasures we've accumulated throughout our lifetimes. Sturdy is no longer our prime concern in making furniture selections. Mouthwash and cleansers are close at hand. Earrings, cufflinks, and loose change may find their homes on dresser tops while knitting or sewing boxes permanently rest next to the television chair. We may find ourselves using real china and crystal more frequently. We have the right to live any way we choose—we've earned it.

Entertaining grandchildren, though, inevitably means making some adjustments to the castle. Before they begin to creep, you must make a conscious decision as to what will be the most comfortable way for you to entertain your young and very curious grandchildren in your home. There are at least two schools of thought on this: hide everything, or teach grandchildren early to respect your things. Whichever method you choose, think preventative

*T*IP: Collect safe plastic or plush toys to put out on your tabletops whenever very young grandchildren visit.

---

caution when preparing your home for a visit with your grandchild. Breakage should not be your only concern. Items that may be ingested, choke, burn, or cut should also be eliminated.

If you subscribe to the "hide everything" philosophy, you can childproof your whole home or several rooms until you feel confident in your grandchild's ability to respect your possessions, or you can do a kamikaze swoop before each visit. Clear tabletops are great for coloring or spreading out books and toys. Don't worry about how neat and tidy the castle remains during grand visits. View fingerprints as youthful decorating touches! Save the cleanup for afterward and focus on enjoying this grandchild's company. You should provide plenty of playthings in every room that your grandchild frequents.

& "I don't get to see my grandchildren very often. I was so nervous that they were going to break something or hurt themselves that I couldn't relax. I hated having to nag them to leave my things alone. I've found that it's just easier for me to put fragile decorations in a box in my bedroom before they visit and then replace them after

they go home. Our visits are much more enjoy-
able now."

—Midge, age 47

Leaving most of your possessions out requires a lot of
patience and vigilance. In order for this to work, your
grandchild must be a frequent visitor to your home. You
must be prepared to teach your grandchild how to look at
and touch your possessions in a positive way, being per-
fectly clear about what he can and cannot do. When
mishaps happen, as they well may, keep cool. If there is
something you absolutely can't live without, you ought to
put it away until your grandchild understands its value.

✎ "I remember taking my young daughter to visit a
grandmotherly friend. This lady had a collection
of beautiful porcelain figurines. As soon as we got
to her house, she took my daughter around to see
them and told her a story about each one. She
emphasized that while they were there for everyone to enjoy looking at, no one was to touch them.
Then she brought out an old suitcase filled with
interesting stuff for a child to play with. Through
the years and with all my other children, the
scenario was always the same. My kids loved
to visit her. She became the grandmother they
didn't have."

—Violette, age 45

Products like laundry detergent, paint, polishes, shampoos, mouthwash, and medicines are toxic. When little ones come to call, supervision is in order to prevent accidental ingestion or burns from common household materials. If you choose, you can purchase a wide variety of locks and latches for cabinets, drawers, and toilets from hardware or baby stores that will secure the storage areas from curious little fingers.

℘ "I think that safety latches are more trouble than they are good. My grandson can open those lids and latches faster than I can. I keep my bedroom and bathroom doors closed when he visits. I even put little hooks up high on the doors to be sure my grandson can't sneak in. I did move most of the cleaning supplies up off the floor so he wouldn't get into them. But, in the end, you really have to watch young children all the time."

—Mary, age 62

It is wise for grandparents to think about their tools and hobbies and their implements in terms of child protection. Instead of hiding your knitting needles, teach your grandchild that one end is sharp and pointy. Let your very young grandchild hold the yarn and wind it around the needles. Share your skills with older grandchildren by showing them how to knit.

℘ "I like to tinker with tools and was worrying about the grandchildren being around hammers and nails. My daughter, the teacher, showed me how to let the little ones hammer golf tees into Styrofoam with wooden mallets first. After a while, they were ready to hammer big-headed nails that were already started into pine blocks. As time went by, it was real easy to work them up to handling other tools. Another thing we did was to get swim goggles for them to use as safety goggles. That helped them to think safety as they handled the tools."

—Gil, age 59

If you have a dog or cat sharing your life, it may not be used to the noise or love assaults of a small child. Pets should be introduced slowly to new folks, especially small, vociferous ones. It is a good idea to ask your adult children if they are apprehensive about Fido or Fluffy getting near the new baby. Animals pick up on tension and fear and react to it. Honestly assess the animal's personality to see if it is asking too much for it to adjust to a very young grandchild. If this is the case, give the animal a break in the backyard or another room while grandchildren visit. When grandchildren are old enough, they can be taught how to approach your pet. Never leave a baby or young child alone in the room with any dog or cat.

TIP: As your grandchild and pet get to know each other, let her help you feed, brush, or exercise your pet.

✒ "Our dog is a very mellow 10-year-old. She has always been around teenagers and adults. We are very careful when our little granddaughter comes around because you just never know about animals. We are helping the baby learn to pat her and to feed her treats. When we can't be with them, we just put the dog outside with a treat so that she isn't jealous. We love that dog, but if she ever snaps at our grandchild, she's history."

—Margaret, age 49

Grandchildren and Medicine

Although you'll probably never have to use them, it's wise to add three telephone numbers to the emergency list by your telephone: your grandchild's pediatrician, the regional poison control center, and your local emergency room. If you will be watching your grandchild while her parents are away, ask for a notarized letter giving you permission to seek medical attention. A true emergency will be handled at the hospital.

Forewarned is forearmed. A basic knowledge of first

aid can come in very handy. Consider taking a CPR course from your local fire department or YMCA. Some hospital pediatric units offer courses in pediatric first aid.

Teach grandchildren how to use medicine appropriately. Never cajole your grandchild into taking medicine by pretending it's candy. Even Mary Poppins gave that spoonful of sugar *after* the medicine went down. Every year, hundreds of small children are rushed to emergency rooms because they have ingested medicine they thought was candy. A wise grandparent will tell a grandchild to take his medicine "because it will help to chase the bad bugs out of his body," not "because it will make him feel better." Explain to your grandchild why you take your medicine. "Sometimes my heart skips a beat. This medicine keeps my heart beating regularly." This makes taking medicine a serious business and reinforces that we only take medicine for serious reasons.

& "On one of my visits to my daughter's home, my two-year-old granddaughter got into my suitcase and found my high blood pressure medicine. Somehow she got the top open and brought it

---

TIP: Check with your local hospital, Red Cross, or firehouse and sign yourself and your older grandchildren up for a first aid course.

upstairs to me. I was so panicked I couldn't remember how many pills I had left in the bottle. I didn't know if she had eaten any or several. We called the poison control center, and thank God, this medication was not considered especially harmful. But we were told to watch her closely for the rest of the day. I was a nervous wreck for the rest of the visit. From then on, I always kept my suitcase locked."

—Jo, age 65

Grandchildren in Cars

When taking car trips, either short or long distance, make sure both you and your grandchild are buckled up. We must vow to be a good role model for our grandchildren from the very beginning. Grandchildren will learn more from what we do than what we say. Not only are child restraints the law in most states, but children who ride in restraints are better behaved than those who do not. If headed on a lengthy trip, a wise grandparent will fight the urge to get from point A to point B as quickly as possible. A good rule of thumb with young children is to stop every forty-five minutes for a break. Make sure to stop somewhere where your grandchild can

*T*IP: Read the owners' manual for your grandchild's safety seat. Be sure you install it correctly in your car. Child safety seats improperly installed become a hazard rather than a safety device.

---

frolic and play safely for ten to fifteen minutes before getting back into the car.

> "My children know that if they get out of their car seats or start a fight in the car, we pull over to the side of the road and stay put until they get straight to travel again. Their grandparents do exactly the same thing if trouble starts. We keep reminding the kids that they know the rules. It helps so much to have their grandparents use the same rules, words, and consequences in dealing with car issues."
>
> —Val, age 34

Grandchildren Outdoors

The outdoor world holds magical discoveries for your grandchild: pretty flowers, soft earth to dig in, thick bushes and shrubs to hide among. The pressures of polite behavior can be left indoors, freeing your grandchild to run, shriek, climb, roll, or dig. Since your grandchild will

TIP: Hide plastic eggs in your yard for your grand-child to find. Include a treat or a note inside.

---

be getting a worm's eye view of your backyard, do a little reconnaissance work before releasing her. Clean up debris, sharp objects, pet droppings, and bird food and feathers. Unless you are including her in the activity, you should also suspend any real-life yard chores and focus attention on having a good time with your grandchild.

To feel truly secure, children need to know their community, not just the house and backyard. It helps to familiarize your grandchild with your neighborhood. Take walks to introduce her to neighbors, friends, and the mail carrier. Show her where the mailbox, park, and other close by landmarks are.

"I want my grandchildren to feel really comfortable when they come to visit us. We take a lot of walks with the grandkids and ask them to plot the route and get us home so they get used to the place. We also have them check for cars before we cross streets and have them tell us when the lights say we can go. As they get older, we plan on letting them be navigator on trips to the supermarket or dry cleaner. I think they'll be safer if they understand where they are."

—Bruce, age 55

Grandchildren and Water

Water is a magnet for young children. It's not just the backyard swimming pool or lily pond that holds danger. The chilling fact is that a young child can drown in less than two inches of water. Grandparents must be on guard when their grandchildren are around any large amounts of water—buckets, tubs, or toilet bowls.

The wonder of water makes baths an enchanting time for babies and toddlers. They so enjoy splashing about that bath time is an exhilarating experience. But you must never, for any reason, leave your grandchild unattended in the tub for even a brief moment. If you are bathing your grandchild in your home, make sure the thermostat on your hot water heater is turned down. Scalding from hot tap water is an easily avoidable accident.

Swimming pools, whether in-ground or inflatable, will provide hours of amusement at Grandma's house. Make sure to stock up on safe water toys for your grandchild. Let her help you put them away so she will not be tempted to wander back alone in search of a favorite pool

---

TIP: Take a water safety class at your local YMCA and invite older grandchildren to take the course with you.

toy. If you have an in-ground pool, keep a shepherd's crook, a life preserver, and a telephone at poolside. Most importantly, an attentive adult should always be present when your grandchild is in the pool. Leave your book or newspaper inside for another day.

Grandchildren in the Real World

As grandchildren grow, their world expands to include the temptations and dangers of modern life. Grandparents must remain vigilant to different issues of child safety while spending time with their grandchildren. While you continue to be guided by the principles of accident prevention and modeling appropriate behaviors, practical grandparenting of school-age grandchildren becomes more interactive. Together you can talk over issues of concern and reach a plan of action.

It is only normal for your grandchild to test his boundaries. Talk with your adult children about what hangouts and friends are acceptable. It is appropriate for your grandchild to clear his plans with you when visiting your home. Although he may protest that you are treating

---

*T*IP: Get to know your grandchild's friends. Allow her to invite friends over to your house for an occasional video and burger.

him like a baby, deep down he knows that your primary concern is for his safety. Carefully monitoring who he is with and where he is going eliminates many potential problems.

Even with the utmost care, trouble can still arise. Grandparents who notice substantive changes in appetite, sleep patterns, hygiene, interest, activity, and general personality traits in their grandchild should be alarmed and involved. Such changes may indicate anything from a temporary funk to serious depression, substance abuse to sexual battery. When the child you know suddenly seems remarkably different, don't wait to find the root cause or hard evidence. Tell your grandchild that you want to help and can if she will let you. Listen hard to anything she tells you. In the same sense of loving concern, alert her parents. Offer to help in any way you can. If it is necessary, you may have to go beyond the family to appropriate social services for information and assistance.

  ⁐ "My grandparents saved my life. My mother's boyfriend wouldn't leave me alone. My mother never noticed the way he was coming on to me, but they

---

𝒯IP: Educate yourself about contemporary teen problems. There are many good books covering the modern teenager's stressful world.

did. They invited me to stay with them for a while, and I finally told them about it. There was a big deal, and I moved in with them permanently. They found a counselor for me. I have just started feeling safe in the last year. I don't know what I might have done if they hadn't acted for me."

—Melissa, age 19

Money and possessions become increasingly important to older grandchildren. Sometimes a grandchild who wants things will connive, lie, or even steal to get them. Grandparents need to use their hard-earned experience to evaluate circumstances as they appear. The grandchild who had five dollars when he left for the mall and came home with three CDs and a T-shirt no doubt has a story to tell. Don't lose your sense of perspective because you so love this child. You might approach this issue with "That must have been some sale. Let's you and I go right back there to get more." Share your concerns with your grandchild and his parents as you see fit. Under such circumstances, it would be wise to watch your wallet and offer your grandchild opportunities to earn money. You need to emphasize your values of fairness and honesty and set a worthy example of integrity. Shower him with positive attention and tell him every good thing you can think of about him. Persistent lying or stealing in older children calls for professional help rather than punishment.

✍ "My grandchild had sticky fingers in a store. Her mother asked me for help. I take her to the dollar store when she visits because she loves to buy little triflin' stuff. I told her straight out, 'You can't leave this store without anything that you don't have a receipt for.' She would show me what she bought and show me the receipt. I told her this every time we went to the store. Now, she says, 'I know, Grandma, I've got to have a receipt for everything.' "

—Pearl, age 50

Teenagers have been known to test limits, take risks, and act without thinking. The consequences of these behaviors are more dangerous today than with any previous generation because of contemporary diseases, violence, and social liabilities. Young people have a hard time obeying what they feel are arbitrary or old-fashioned rules. As grandparents, we aren't the rule makers, but we can make sure we know and support the rules. We can concentrate on setting an example that is worth following, being absolutely clear about our values and following them. We can emphasize personal choice and responsibility for personal consequences.

TIP: If you want someone to emulate your values, then you have to set a good example and live by those values.

Grandchildren and
Life-Threatening Dangers

The greatest percentage of new smokers in the United States are teenage girls. Despite the surgeon general's warning and a multitude of studies linking smoking to cancer, heart disease, and other health problems, smoking is on the rise among adolescents. The social pressure to smoke, especially in high school, is staggering. If you would rather not see your grandchildren become addicted, don't model the behavior, be permissive, or make it easy for them to smoke in your home. If they want to quit, offer all the support you can to help them do it.

🌿 "I started to smoke around 15. My parents went nuts and were all over me about it. I rebelled even more, and we had some pretty terrible fights about it.

"I went to spend a month with my grandparents. They never nagged but told me that they loved me too much to allow me to hurt myself when they were around. They allowed no smoking on their property, inside or out. They knew it was a hard habit to break, however; they kept dishes of candy and gum and pretzels in every room. I think they dreamed up ways to keep my hands busy because I did a lot of projects that month.

"After about ten days, I started to believe them when they told me I didn't need cigarettes any more. By the time I went home, I told my parents I had decided to quit all by myself and had done so without much help. I never did tell them the truth about how I stopped smoking."

—Shelley, age 18

Many adults are amazed to learn that age 10 is the time most children first experiment with alcohol. This is a problem that grows enormously as children move through middle school and high school. Some sobering thoughts: most teenagers today drink for the purpose of getting drunk, and those who drink do so more than once a week. You must make sure your message emphasizing responsible decision making is loud and clear. Drinking and driving is illegal and deadly. No one should ever drive after drinking.

🖎 "We have always had beer and wine in our home and at our table. We always offered a taste to the young folks. I recently realized that I need to watch how much I drink when my grandson is around. I don't want to give him the wrong idea."

—Jim, age 52

To a teenager, nothing is more eagerly anticipated than getting that driver's license. It signals a coming of age, a new freedom. A group of teenagers, a fast car, and

*T*IP: **Finance an accident avoidance course for your newly licensed grandteen.**

---

lack of judgment conjure images that strike terror in the heart of even the most easygoing of adults. By age 13 your grandteen will be chomping at the bit to get behind the wheel of a car. You can let your teenage grandchild help you tinker with the car and help wash and wax it. When driving, talk safety and defensive driving strategies. You will have a captive audience.

✍ "Our grandchildren are getting close to driving age. I try to explain why I do certain things when I drive. Kids learn better when you tell them why. The 15-year-old is now very interested in how I drive. It gives me the chance to teach his mind a bit before he gets behind the wheel. We also have lots to talk about when we ride together."

—Al, age 59

Almost every day we read about the effect of drugs on escalating crime, schooling, and family life. The prevalence of drugs in our society is on the rise. As grandparents, we want to do everything possible to keep our grandchildren safe from the plague of drugs. Examine your own medication usage. Are you careful and precise in medication usage?

Do you seek professional advice or do you self-medicate? Have you purged your medicine cabinet of outdated or unnecessary prescriptions? You need to think about how you use or depend upon drugs. Would your grandchild think that on a regular basis you need drugs to sleep, to feel happy, to cope? Do you model alternatives such as fresh air, exercise, laughter, hard work, rest, or relaxation techniques instead of pill swallowing to relieve stress?

> ✍ "Our granddaughter put herself in the hospital twice because she overused her asthma medication. The family didn't see that she was using her prescription to try to make herself happier—not just for breathing. We all had to take a good look at how we used medicines ourselves and what kind of message we were giving her."
>
> —Peter, age 59

When our grandchildren are seeking relief from their troubles, some of them turn to drugs that alter their mood. Some have found they need to look no further than their own home to find that high. The abuse of inhalants, especially among the preteen group, is increasing at an alarming level. Inhaling substances like glues, propellants (like those found in whipping cream), paints, and thinners are often overlooked because they are so readily available. For the very same reasons, some children may choose to abuse over-the-counter substances like mouthwash and

---

$\mathcal{T}$IP: Look for movies that explore complex issues faced by young adults. Take your grandchild to these movies and discuss the movies afterward at a favorite restaurant.

---

cough medicine, both of which have a very high alcohol content. We need to be aware of our grandchildren's sense of well-being as well as their social habits. When we see a problem in either that is beyond our loving touch, we need to reach out to find help elsewhere for the kids we love.

Eating disorders present yet another potential problem. In a society that emphasizes skinny models and media stars, it is natural that adolescents searching for perfection turn to dieting as a way of life. For some it becomes a road to death. Anorexia, amateur vegetarianism, and bulimia all occur in young people, most often our granddaughters. It never works to *tell* them they are "just right"; we have to make them *feel* "just right."

$\mathcal{L}\heartsuit$ "We were very worried about our daughter's dieting habits when she was around 14. As parents, we were on her all the time. We had our family doctor talk to her, and many family friends did, too. My parents found a healthy eating/weight reduction course at a local hospital and invited her to enroll with them (even though Grandma weighed all of

104 pounds). That worked. She began to eat more sensibly and exercise regularly."

—Marilyn, age 51

Every teenage generation has its struggle with a moral dilemma. Today's teens are bombarded with innumerable messages regarding sex. They joke and taunt each other about it. It can be treated as a precious privilege or a randy rite of passage.

🖘 "My grandfather was the ultimate gentleman. He held doors for anyone, would offer his seat to a woman long after it wasn't acceptable to do that. He always held Nana's chair and had his sons and grandsons do the same for female family and guests.

"I once told him an off-color joke. He didn't like it. He told me he loved women and that loving women was no laughing matter. I felt like a bug. He made a big impression on how I learned to feel about women."

—Jerry, 31

Sex can mean many things—it embraces sexuality, sexual harassment, homosexuality, and sex education. It includes the issues of sexually transmitted disease, AIDS, rape, abortion, condom distribution, right to life, teenage pregnancy, unwed motherhood and fatherhood—all issues that deeply affect our national quality of life. They just as surely touch many, many of our grandchildren. Teens are justifiably confused and concerned. Many are very willing to talk out their confusion with a responsible adult who's not quite as close as a parent. This is especially true when a loving grandparent opens the door to discussing controversial issues. Stories in newspapers, legislation, and themes of TV shows can be used to start a good dialogue that helps teens refine their attitudes and broaden their perspectives. The essential ingredient in such a situation is respect for each other's point of view. When adults take teens seriously and respect their opinions, even while disagreeing with them, the path is paved for moral and ethical development. Wise grandparents know this kind of informed, unemotional give-and-take discussion can help cement the values we hold so dearly.

Although we cannot single-handedly cure all of our society's ills, we can be very sure that the customs and values we demonstrate to and with our grandchildren will become ones that foster responsibility and appropriate loving behavior. At each and every stage, grandparents can provide the wise avenue that prevents disaster.

9

A Very Merry Unbirthday

❖

Celebrating Occasions
Great and Small

The Mad Hatter was a child's kind of guy. Not content to wait for the calendar to order a celebration, he jumped at the slightest opportunity to throw an unbirthday party. Life never got too mundane for the Mad Hatter. He was blessed with a child's capacity to celebrate the moment.

Human beings have an innate need to occasionally jump for joy. The impulse goes back to the cave people, who turned a productive hunting or fishing trip into a dance around the camp fire. Modern people, unfortunately, go about celebration in an orderly, consumer-oriented way, setting aside specific days on the calendar to kick up their heels and celebrate turning points in the seasonal or religious calendar. As adults, we are burdened by the jobs of menu planning, invitations, and decorations that rob our celebration of childlike spontaneity. Grandparenting allows us to reconnect through our grandchildren with the wonder of holidays and celebrations.

Sharing the joy of a child opening a present, watching a parade, gazing wide-eyed at candles on a cake or fireworks exploding in the night sky gives all of us back the magic of celebrations. The Christmas, Hanukkah, or Kwanzaa celebrations that we orchestrate for our grandchildren will provide some of their warmest family memories. How we approach the idea of celebration will influence the way future generations are able to come together in joy to mark the large and small triumphs of family.

    "For some reason that I don't even understand today, my family never celebrated anything. Religious holidays were observed in church, but the family observance was muted and stingy. I really missed that feeling of group celebration. With my own family, I have tried to instill a sense of celebration and joy. We started our own Christmas traditions, like baking special bread, going together to Midnight Mass, and coming home to open one present and share that special bread. I want to be sure that my grandchildren find a joyous family ready to celebrate the big moments in life together."

—Adam, age 55

TI P : **Resurrect the fondest memories of family times from your childhood and tailor them to this generation. Set up a puzzle table with an ongoing one-thousand-piece puzzle; play penny poker or charades together.**

Coming together to celebrate with family and friends and catch up on new times and old times is the essence of holiday celebrations. Each of these gatherings provides our grandchildren with a deeper understanding of who they are. Traditions, ethnic dishes, and conversations in native tongue (either shared or overheard) imprint our culture on our grandchildren. Seldom-seen relatives, from eccentric old Aunt Esther to wild and woolly Cousin Sam, bring life to the family tree.

In today's mobile and fast-paced society, it's often difficult for families to gather as frequently as they once did. When the opportunity for a celebration arrives, it is doubly precious.

Celebrations have many faces. Those marking major life events—weddings, christenings, graduations, confirmations, bar or bat mitzvahs—mark the personal milestones in our family's history. They are the most intensely personal celebrations on our calendars. These rites of passage usually demand the most heroic planning, delve into our deepest traditions, and reward us with the most enduring family memories. Family and friends from far

TIP: Take a photo of your family at least once a year. Keep everyone in the same positions year after year so they can compare growth and change over the years.

and near journey together to celebrate our personal family milestone.

    "At our family weddings, just before the meal, the eldest male, now my grandfather, says a blessing. Then he cuts challah for all the guests to share. It is a very old eastern European tradition that signifies good luck to the bride and groom."

—Saul, age 27

The birth of a new family member is an occasion to celebrate and a good time to help sibling grandchildren prepare a welcome for their new brother or sister. While parents and new baby are resting and settling in, give your older grandchild the responsibility for notifying cousins far and wide about the new arrival. She can design, address, and mail personalized birth announcements to distant family and friends. Your grandchild can make a booklet telling her new baby brother or sister what was happening the day he was born in the world outside and in the family. It will be a wonderful keepsake for the family and the child. Such activities help make your grandchild feel important and an active part of the growing family. Grandparents who can help in this way often prevent the feelings of loneliness and jealousy that can mar a new baby's homecoming.

Making a little extra effort to continue family traditions surrounding these events provides a sense of family in a more and more impersonal society.

🖉 "Our family has an heirloom christening dress. It has been worn by everyone in our family for generations. The new mother writes her baby's name on the long slip and then embroiders it—pink for girls and blue for boys. Dressing my new baby in something touched by so many generations was a very sentimental thing."

—Dottie, age 23

Family reunions are a wonderful way to bridge distance and time and reinvigorate a family's sense of being a unique unit, a wonderful "us." Reunions require someone to take the initiative, contact the entire family, and coordinate the events. Grandparents are logical candidates for this job.

Because it can take from six months to a year to plan a successful reunion, they are not common occurrences. Many hands can make lighter work of the details and infuse the celebration with a wider spectrum of family imprints. They are most successful if you plan far enough

TIP: Create a family cookbook with contributions from everyone. Reproduce it and send copies to all family members. Update the cookbook as the family grows.

---

ahead so that all family members can schedule it on their calendars. Lodging is the first big hurdle. Very few people have homes large enough to house a full family reunion. Consider booking accommodations in a state park or resort in a central location for the far-flung family. Many of these facilities are geared to families and offer activities to keep all ages occupied—swimming, hiking, tennis, boating, horseback riding—often at reduced group rates. A central location lifts the burden of hospitality from any one relative and portions it equally among family members. Consider purchasing visible symbols or keepsakes of the event: caps or T-shirts emblazoned with "Smith Family Reunion, 1995"; a catchy family slogan; or the names of everyone in attendance.

Include activities that are fun and relaxing for all and don't forget quiet time for the individual families to explore, sightsee, or rest. Teens should feel comfortable choosing between adult or child activities. Plan on dividing the cost, transportation, and responsibilities in a way that enables all to participate with enthusiasm.

Once the stuff of warm family memories and traditions, seasonal and religious holidays are now a marketing tool. It's easy to get caught up in the frenzied advertising and hype surrounding holiday buying and preparation or become so wearied by the commercialism that you stop looking forward to the holiday itself. What are our memories of great holiday celebrations? What probably sticks in most of our minds is who was there and what they said and did, the closeness of decorating or preparing food together, or performing an individual family ritual. You need to take the reins again and make your holiday celebrations your very own without worrying about whether they stand up to glossy magazine spreads or TV hype.

Involve your grandchild in the traditional flavor of the holiday by giving him a part in orchestrating it. If he lives nearby, invite him over the day before the big event to help you decorate and complete last-minute preparations. If he has his driver's license, he probably would be happy to run some errands for you. If your grandchildren are journeying to be with you, save some preparations for them. Older children can make the holiday punch, little ones can pass the hors d'oeuvres. This gives us the oppor-

---

*T*IP: Young grands might enjoy trimming a tree for the birds. Get together scooped-out orange halves filled with peanut butter and cornmeal (mixed half and half) and pine cones rolled in the same mixture, then in birdseed. Let the children go outside and trim an evergreen shrub.

tunity to share the stories behind the traditions and rituals of our celebrations and weave our grandchildren into the performance of our patterns and heritage.

&❤ "My grandparents invite the whole family and anyone's friends to come and decorate their home on Christmas Eve. Every imaginable decoration is set out, and we go wild with lights, wreaths, and bows. We move furniture and put up two trees. The kids mostly decide how to do it, and my grandparents go along with the plans. Nannie fixes special food for snacking, including her famous cheese goo. Every year it is sort of the same, and every year it sort of changes. Christmas Eve is the one event of the year that I would not want to miss."

—Jessie, age 18

Since families are so far-flung and busy, it's easy to go overboard with festivities by trying to cram all the memories you can into one day or week during the year. Keep in mind as you plan that the celebration must fit the celebrants. When your grandchild is very small, too much food, too many decorations, and too many new faces or long rituals are overwhelming. Plan your celebration with your youngest grandchild in mind. Elaborate meals that stretch into the evening are guaranteed to cause the disintegration of a young child. It's a better idea to simplify the meal and rituals and spend most of your time visiting with this much-missed family unit.

Your adolescent grandchild may need a little coaxing to rejoin the group. Adolescents and adults keep an uneasy truce at the best of times. Welcome your adolescent grandchild dressed all in black and sporting combat boots with the same enthusiasm that you welcome your three-year-old granddaughter garbed in ruffles and Mary Janes. Do you have current pictures displayed of every grandchild? Often we concentrate on the cuteness of our young grandchild and take for granted that our older grandchildren know we love them. All of your grandchildren need to be active participants. Provide your adolescent grandchild with a disposable camera so she can be the official photographer of the event. This allows her to participate and stand on the edges at the same time if she wants.

Hoarding our jubilation for a picture-perfect occasion some ten days a year is too miserly an approach. Every day is special. As adults, we often lose track of that. We need to celebrate the little things in life because they are the building blocks of the large things. Since we spend official time commemorating, memorializing, observing, inaugurating, or ritualizing holidays others have chosen, we certainly have the right to invent our own personal holidays. Inventing a special holiday with our grandchild lets him know just how special he is.

Declare a holiday for the first robin sighting, the first

day of school, a winter picnic, or the first snowfall. Choose a milestone in your grandchild's life and celebrate together—the day she got her driver's license, the day she entered first grade, the day she mastered tying her shoes.

✍ "My grandparents always take our whole family out to eat on the first and last day of school. We go some place fun and get to tell all about our new teachers and stuff. We tell funny stories about kids and teachers. I really like this because it makes starting and stopping school special. None of my friends do this. It's just my grandparents' thing."
—Suzanne, age 10

Everyone loves surprise packages. Long-distance grandparents can send baskets of food out of the blue to celebrate any of these small family occasions. Send a disposable camera and a mailer so you can share the memories. Comparing the first fish you catch in the spring and the first fish your grandchild lands can become a fun competition over the years. Take pictures and exchange

---

*T*IP: Get a calendar of upcoming events in your locale and give the listing to your grandchild. Let him choose an activity that you can attend together. If the first is successful, make a tradition out of it.

them and make bets on who will make the first strike next year.

Each of us has developed some minitraditions within our own families as they grew. We may not even be aware of them, but these traditions spill over into your grown child's family, bringing the spirit of their grandparents into the intimate life of their grandchild. The little things repeated are often what make children feel most secure and genuinely a part of a family. Tea and graham crackers in the evening using special mugs or cups can become something remembered when life gets hard or lonely. If you did it for your own children and they remember it fondly, you will see it crop up in the routine of their own families.

> "My gran has a little china jar with a lid on it. She keeps it on a shelf in the dining room. Whenever one of us would cry, she would run and get the "tear jar" and try to catch our tears. We came to see tears as too precious to waste. The whole deal of capturing and storing tears would have us laughing so fast. It was such a neat trick that I have my own special tear jar on the mantelpiece in my home."
>
> —Cindy, age 32

Vacations used to be long, hazy days of discovery and free time when families came together and relaxed during school vacations. That is not possible for many today. More school systems are changing to a year-round schedule where there is no big summer break. Sometimes children's neighborhood pals are not even on the same schedule, leaving their families scrambling to find companions and fill free time.

Knowing your grandchildren's schedule allows you to plan times when you can fill a void in their activities with short trips or extended visits to Gran's house.

✍ "I recently sat next to two young kids on an airplane, a young boy about seven and his younger sister. They had what looked like a butterfly net that the boy was holding throughout the trip. I asked them where they were going. 'To our grandparents house for a couple of weeks,' the boy said. 'We're going to catch fireflies. You do still have fireflies, don't you?' he asked. I assured him that there were still plenty of fireflies back East. When we got off the plane, they ran into their grandparents' arms and the little boy waved the firefly net at his grandfather, 'See, Grandpop, I got a firefly net.' He was so excited. It kinda gave me a warm feeling."

—Jake, age 46

If you and your grandchild have a brief period of free time that coincides, why not take a short trip together?

Many hotels offer weekend packages that could be just the ticket. In addition to the fun of staying some place other than home, these weekends could include meals in ethnic restaurants, museums, theaters, offbeat shopping, and a dab of sightseeing. Consider the age of your grandchild in your plans. A young child may not need to go any further than the hotel swimming pool, whereas you and your teenage grandchild might prefer to paint the town together.

Longer stretches of time allow you to consider prepaid packages to resorts, dude ranches, farms, and cruises. The diversity of activities provided in these packages relieves you of planning hassles. Beach vacations are often the perfect choice on or off season.

As your grandchild approaches his teens, consider taking him with you when you travel for work. Your adolescent grand will love the chance to sleep in while you work, and can shop or exercise in the afternoon and meet you for dinner and a show. Allow some private time for both yourself and your grandchild. One of the bonuses of sharing business travel is letting your grandchild see your business persona, which adds a richness and texture to your portrait.

TIP: If you earn frequent-flyer miles, send some to your older grandchild so she can meet you after a business trip. Use the weekend to explore the town.

✍ "My grandma is vice president of a big university. She spends a lot of time traveling to conferences and meetings. Sometimes she takes me with her. I have gone to California, New Orleans, Wyoming, and even on a cruise to Mexico with her. While she's in meetings, all of us kids have planned activities like crafts, Ping-Pong tournaments, swimming, and games with counselors. I've met kids from all over the country. I even write to some of them. Then when she's finished work, we usually do some fun things together. She has a way of making you feel sooo special."

—Courtney, age 13

Lots of the activities that are available in your area are food for grandchild fun. Summer fairs, autumn wine stompings, apple and pumpkin picking, candlelight tours in winter, all offer an opportunity to turn free time into memorable time.

✍ "My grandad started taking me to the county fair when I was just a little kid. We had a regular thing to spend the day, eat cotton candy, watch tractor pulls, check the livestock, and at the very end do the rides. We moved away when I was ten, but each year I go back to do the fair with him. It's not the fair that I look forward to now, it's visiting with him."

—Chuck, age 20

*T*IP: Give a "half birthday" party for your young grandchild. If his real birthday is in December, have a funny, silly half birthday in June.

Taking a cue from the Mad Hatter, we need to step off society's hectic track to celebrate the sublime and the goofy in our own individual manner. Celebrate together the solemn and the traditional. Take time out to acknowledge the mini-triumphs and dispel the doldrums in your family with a joyous unholiday. Don't let the essence of celebration slip through the cracks of busy schedules and commercialism. Families need to make joy together; it is an essential food for family.

10

Happily Ever After

❖

Carrying Our Heritage
into the Future

A gentle sigh escapes as the storyteller reaches the words "and they lived happily ever after" at the close of a fairy tale. Magic of some sort has enabled the hero or heroine to conquer tremendous odds, and right has prevailed. Modern children never tire of these stories no matter how old-fashioned they are.

Grandparents are the storytellers of our families. That role is just as important today as it was when families first came together as tribes. The tribal storyteller was entrusted with the oral history of the tribe. He or she clarified for the children, through ritual stories, all that was important to culture and survival. As the modern family has scattered across the continent and the world, time for absorbing those tales is evaporating.

Some of us have a box of sepia photos of unknown relatives in our attic. By now, it may be too late to learn their identities and what they contributed to our heritage. They will remain mysterious men and women staring out of history at their bemused great-great-grandchildren. We have lost forever a piece of ourselves. Don't let that happen to your grandchildren. Tell them your tales.

🖉 "I'm going to ask something of every one of you. Let me start with my generation, the grandparents out there. You are our living link to the past. Tell your grandchildren the story of the struggles waged, at home and abroad; of sacrifices freely made for freedom's sake. And tell them your own story as well— because every American has a story to tell."
—George Bush, State of the Union Address, 1990

Grandparents can weave magic into the fabric of our families in the stories that we tell our grandchildren. We know all the Jacks in our family who slew giants. We know all the clever Gretels and the Hansels that they saved. We can tell real-life tales of symbolic dragons slain and straw spun into gold. We also know the tales of the highwaymen and the foolish fishermen in our family history. Unlike fairy tales, our folk created their own magic from the seeds of their heritage and their hopes.

When we transmit our heritage to our grandchildren, we are casting them in a never-ending story of family that

*T*IP: **Learn the traditions of new family members. Ask for recipes and activities. Try out new ideas and celebrate holidays by melding your in-laws' traditions with your own.**

---

will bolster their own efforts to conquer ogres and separate the real human values from the dross of pop culture.

Our grandchildren need to know where they came from—what frogs and princes inhabit their family line. They need to participate fully in the traditions of family and join in the joyous coming together of all its separate entities in times of celebration. Our grandchildren's sense of family stability and strength comes from this history and practice. Grandparents are central in gluing all the different factions of the family together. Our grandchildren can then ride the wings of family into their own happily-ever-after.

"My grandfather told me that one of my distant ancestors was a pirate. As a child, I made up wonderful stories about 'my pirate.' I used him over and over again in school and to impress my friends. My children have come to know the pirate very well. While we don't even know his name, he is our most infamous relative. I could hardly wait to pass him on to my own grandchildren."

—Blanche, age 67

Family history gives our grandchildren a chance to lift their own families above the mundane. When our grandchildren learn of relatives that were the original inhabitants of this land or those that came here either willingly or unwillingly, it places our family in the history of our country. When we relate to our grandchildren the struggles our forebears overcame to find their place in America, they begin to learn appreciation and tolerance for the new Americans that reach our shores daily. We can spark an interest in our grandchildren in the culture from which we came—Irish, Mexican, Chinese, Indian, African. We can share our own memories of the traditions that our ancestors held—the kinds of food our grandmothers made, the family heirlooms that were passed down to us, the political and religious ideas that were instilled in us. We may not continue them today, but they are a conscious or subconscious part of what we are. And they will influence our grandchildren, too.

✑ "My grandfather was one of Teddy Roosevelt's Rough Riders. Recently, my granddaughter had to write a report for school on some part of American history. I told her about my grandfather, and

---

*T*IP: Plan a trip with your grandchild to touch your family's roots. You might go to Ellis Island, the old neighborhood, or even the old country.

we made a trip to Arlington Cemetery to view his grave. It was an amazing feeling standing there amongst all those white crosses with two generations paying homage to a third. We went to the library and got some books on the Rough Riders and found my grandfather's name in one of the books. It was a great report—for both of us."

—Ted, age 54

The heirlooms we keep are touchstones to the past. They show us how far we have come and how close we still remain to the personalities and tastes of those who gave us our genetic makeup. They link us to those who came before us and make family history a personal and touchable thing.

"I can remember visiting my grandmother's house. It was full of things. She had a cut-glass perfume jar that I loved. She would take it down from the place of honor and let me hold it. She told me it was made by her French grandfather, who was a glass cutter. He came to this country with nothing, and he could neither read nor write, but he made beautiful things. I was amazed at that because my grandmother had a Ph.D. in math. I would hold that perfume jar in my hands and imagine a clever man with twinkling eyes who made beautiful things. My grandmother left that

jar to me. Now I let my children hold that precious jar and tell them about my great-great-
grandfather."

—Lucy, age 36

Out of the history of our family comes the traditional
ways we have of doing things. Do we traditionally gather
for a meal on Saturdays or Sundays? Do we sing together at
family gatherings? Are we a family that likes to hike? Do
we read voraciously and argue politics? Are we an outdoor
family, a cerebral family, or an artistic family? Our genetic
pool has bubbled together to produce a way of looking at
and enjoying the world that is a blend of all of our past
experiences.

Our family will change as new cultures and traditions
are added by new family members. Family is a very flexible
institution that endures and continually strengthens itself
by the addition of new members and the wealth of tradition and heritage that they bring.

"My wife's family celebrates Hanukkah and mine
celebrates Christmas. For several years, we celebrated both holidays with the appropriate in-laws
and changed decorations in between so as not to
offend anyone. Last year when the whole family,
both sides, was together for Thanksgiving, my
grandmother gave us a wall hanging that she had
made. She insisted that we unwrap it right then. It

was a beautiful stitched picture that incorporated symbols of both holy holidays. It now hangs year-round in our living room. It reminds me that we can keep our heritage and still respect that of the ones we love."

—Jack, age 47

Practically all Americans came to this land from somewhere else. We all blended our various heritages into a working unit. And within each family we have blended many different heritages together. We can make our grandchildren aware of the heritage with which we are most familiar. This can be accomplished without placing the value of one heritage over another, through stories, books, and activities that are shared with our grandchildren. Then, we can try to learn together about our lineage.

When your grandchildren are young, you can give them picture books about the folk heroes from different countries that explain the myths and legends of different

---

TIP: Go to the library with your grandchild and research how all the different cultures in your family celebrate one particular holiday. Choose the parts from each that you like best and plan a new kind of family celebration.

cultures. Celebrate St. David's Day when the daffodils bloom if you are Welsh. Or mark St. Patrick's Day by baking Irish soda bread if your roots are Irish.

✍ "My family is American now. We still have some of our traditions, although they've been kind of Americanized, too. My favorite is the red egg party. In China, so many babies died that their birth was not celebrated until they were several months old. When our new grandchild becomes four months old, we have a red egg party and invite all of our friends to welcome the new baby. We shave the baby's head, dye eggs red for luck, and fix special foods. I have done this for all of my grandchildren."

—June, age 69

As your grandchild grows older, you can expand your heritage activities and have a good time together. If local Scottish festivals are held in your area, take your grandchild to witness and enjoy the flavor of the event. Visit a Jamaican, Afghani, or Mexican restaurant. Better yet, prepare a special ethnic meal with your grandchild, and when he is proficient in the kitchen, give him the recipe.

In addition to the history and celebrations, every culture has its own unique traditions. Some of these traditions surround national feast days, and some are everyday occurrences. Your grandchildren will enjoy taking part in these traditions and learning new rituals. In this way, they are participating in our life and our view of the world in a very personal way.

℘ "My grandmother came to this country from Germany when she was a young woman. She married and raised a family here but continued to practice many of the old traditions. She always put real candles on the Christmas tree. They would be lit on Christmas Eve and the whole family would sing carols and share gifts. Of course, great care was taken to prevent fire and the candles only burned for a very short time. My earliest memories are about candles and being in the circle of my family on Christmas Eve. It never mattered that electric lights have replaced candles in Germany."
—Isabel, age 19

A tradition can be something as profound as a religious ceremony or as personal as Great-aunt Nettie's crystal toothpick holder on the dining room table. It can be a custom that has been passed down from generation to generation or something started for your branch of the family because it fits. Traditions bind families together across and through generations.

℘ "We go out of the city to visit my grandparents at their weekend farm as often as we can. Life is so different there that we have wonderful times. My nana has a lot of funny things that she likes to do. One of them is measuring the grandchildren's bodies against the corn as it grows. When we were little, we couldn't understand how it could get so tall so fast. Pretty soon she is going to have her first great-grandchild, and I'll bet she and I both measure the newest family member against each season's corn."

—Pauline, age 25

Resurrect an old family tradition or custom that may have fallen by the wayside and continue it for your grandchildren. Or invent a tradition that fits this particular grandchild. If you have a special cup handed down to you from your parents or grandparents, make it her special cup at your house and tell her about its history. If it is a tradition for Grandpa to light the first fire in the winter, save that tradition to share with your grandchild.

🙋 "In our family we had a fancy plate that was passed down through several generations. Whenever a child had done something special, that plate was at his place at the table. When something special happened to our parents, we kids would get that plate out for them, too. For last Mother's Day, my grandmother sent me a red plate with the words

'You Are Special Today' written around the rim.
It's going to be the special plate in our family."
—Ellen, age 39

Sometimes traditions are built around the way we
spend our leisure time. We read after dinner, or we take a
nightly walk. Include your grandchild in these simple
daily rituals. They become a part of the day that is
scheduled for closeness.

❧ "I spent a lot of time with a Mormon family while
I was growing up. I always liked the idea of a
'family home evening.' So when we had kids, we
made it a tradition in our home, too. We would
play board games, talk about life, and the kids
would make everybody a snack. Our children are
all grown up and have families of their own now
and they still have family home evening. Whenever we can, we love to be with them on those
evenings."
—Ed, age 63

Some traditions we see in a family are unique to the
family members at that time and place. They are not easily
replicated by future generations in just the same way.
However, the warmth behind that little tradition remains
with us and makes us strive to develop that same warmth
in a way that suits our own family.

𝒯IP: Find an outrageous hat. Take a picture of your-self wearing it. Send the picture and hat to your grandchildren. Have them send a picture of them-selves in the hat to the next grandchild.

✍ "My grandfather always wore a hat. When he came home from anywhere, he would toss that hat into the house before he came in. He always said that if it came back out, he would know not to enter. My grandmother would come to the door laughing and give him a big hug and his hat back. They have been married for over forty years and this hat thing still goes on. It's like an endless joke that all of us are in on."

—Roger, age 20

We can start traditions that are homey and warm and make our grandchildren feel welcome in our lives. Sharing the Sunday comics together, saying a grandparent-grandchild grace before meals, taking a walk to a special place together—all of these things spring from our com-mitment and love for our grandchild. They will reminisce about these small everyday rituals when they are grown and read the Sunday papers to their own children.

✍ "When I visited my gram, we would do the dishes together after dinner. We'd talk and laugh. When the job was finished, we would go outside and sit

*T*IP: Many newspapers publish children's pages in the Sunday papers. Save these to read together with your grandchild.

---

on the porch and watch the stars. She'd put her arm around me, and we'd just sit for a while. That is my warmest, strongest memory of my gram."

—Rebecca, age 29

Happily, grandparenting is an expansive role that gives us the right, the power, and the privilege to influence the shape of our family now and in generations to come. It is a role that answers a genuine need in our world. We owe it to ourselves and to our families to accept the magic mantle of grandparent and provide the leadership, compassion, and peace that we have gained through our life experiences at our own family's hearth. Hand in hand with our grandchildren, we can exercise the muscles of family. Exploring, discovering, reassuring, sheltering, celebrating, this new generation expands the capacity of family to meet and conquer the future. It places the magic of our touch on our family's happily-ever-after.